Stanley Newman's

LITERARY CROSSWORDS

THE PLAY'S THE THING

Random House
Puzzles & Games

ISBN: 0-8129-3527-6

Random House Puzzles & Games Web site address:
www.puzzlesatrandom.com

Manufactured in the United States of America

2 4 6 8 9 7 5 3 1

First Edition

INTRODUCTION

Welcome to *The Play's the Thing*, the first crossword book (as far as we know) whose themes are devoted to plays and playwrights.

Forty of the 50 puzzles each highlight a different play, ranging from the 16th to the 20th century. Eminent playwrights are the themes of the remaining ten. To enhance your enjoyment, each puzzle includes a quotation from the play (or the playwright's debut), plus some interesting trivia, and there are many hundreds of nontheme literary clues throughout the book. If you're a fan of trivia in general, I commend to your attention the Random House book *10,000 Answers: The Ultimate Trivia Encyclopedia*, coauthored by yours truly, in which many of these facts first appeared.

For their help in the preparation of this book, I would like to thank Sandy Fein, my Random House editor, and Jon Delfin, for his thorough proofreading of the manuscript.

Your comments on any aspect of this book are most welcome. You can reach me via regular mail or e-mail at the addresses below.

If you're on e-mail, I invite you to join "Fans of Stan," a free service that will keep you abreast of my activities in the puzzle world: when new books of mine are published, seminars and tournaments I'm conducting, etc. Simply e-mail me at StanXwords@aol.com.

Best wishes for happy solving!

Stan Newman

Regular mail: P.O. Box 69, Massapequa Park, NY 11762
(Please enclose a self-addressed stamped envelope if you'd like a reply)

E-mail: StanXwords@aol.com

---

1 ARSENIC AND OLD LACE (1941)

"Insanity runs in my family. It practically gallops."

ACROSS

1 Coffee brewer
4 Expanse of land
9 Fairy-tale surname
14 Born: Fr.
15 Nancy's rich friend
16 Machine part
17 "__ Got a Crush on You"
18 Devoured
19 Dizzying drawings
20 12 Down's brother, in his own mind
23 Oscar winner as Disraeli
24 Halogen suffix
25 Second-sequel indicator
27 Germ of an idea
28 Rights org.
30 River blockers
31 Salinger title character
33 Part of the eye
35 Setting of the play
40 Waiting room
41 Ocean motion
42 Concerning
43 Astronomical bear
45 American Legion members
49 *Leave __ to Heaven*

50 Western Indian
51 Like some food
53 One of 12 Down's aunts
57 *Full House* actor
58 Farm-equipment name
59 Dictator Amin
60 Singer Cara
61 Holmes' __ *Venner*
62 Tease
63 __ Cup (golf prize)
64 Sized up
65 Compass pt.

DOWN

1 Quarterback great Johnny
2 Longfellow subject
3 *Eye of the __* (Follett novel)
4 Playing cards
5 Crowd sounds
6 Diva's voice range
7 Marc's love, for short
8 Adenoid neighbor
9 Music-dictionary compiler
10 Weapon in Clue
11 Napoli native

12 Main character of the play
13 *The A-Team* star
21 Performed
22 Drew forth
26 Karen Blixen alias
28 One of the Marches
29 Word on a nickel
30 Sec
31 Hosp. chart
32 Anthony Shaffer play
34 Be indebted to
35 Uninspiring
36 Cooking herb
37 More than miffed
38 Yoko __
39 Singer Peeples
44 First-grade book
45 Video format
46 Uncut
47 Made a connection
48 Amanuensis
50 Out-and-out
51 Like Gothic novels
52 Thomas Nast target
54 Philosopher Descartes
55 Composer Bartók
56 Vacation purpose
57 Army title

The
medium
of the
poisonings
is
elderberry
wine.

2 BLITHE SPIRIT (1941)

"It's discouraging to think how many people are shocked by honesty and how few by deceit."

ACROSS

1 Maxwell Perkins, for one
7 Carson sidekick
14 Type of rifle
15 Bach work
16 Walter Mitty type
17 Walked leisurely
18 Subject of the play
20 *And Then There Were* __
21 Lyricist's stock-in-trade
25 Trinidad neighbor
29 Greek peak
31 Fictional Harrington
32 ". . . __ saw Elba"
33 *Peter Pan* dog
35 Circle lines
37 With 39 Across, original portrayer of 54 Across
39 See 37 Across
41 "__ porridge hot . . ."
42 *Green Mansions* character
44 Not fooled by
45 Numerical prefix
46 Jessica's husband
48 In __ by itself
50 *Adaptation* actress
52 Mongkut's governess
54 Medium in the play
60 Generous
63 Glad
64 Italian port
65 "The flower of my heart"
66 Edicts
67 *Will Rogers Follies* prop

DOWN

1 Tombstone lawman
2 Three: Ger.
3 Construction girder
4 Comedian's concern
5 Even odds
6 "Encore performance"
7 1950, on cornerstones
8 They're found in lofts
9 Kaufman collaborator
10 "You __ Sunshine"
11 It's found in lofts
12 Bullfight cheer
13 Nemo's harpooner
14 LP descendants
19 Geologic time unit
22 Muslim holy city
23 Boots out
24 Alternative to Bulovas
25 __ *fugit*
26 Become accustomed
27 Ritzy L.A. suburb
28 Helps
30 Well-grounded
34 __ *Bede*
36 GI offense
38 Prepare for opening night
40 *The Apple Tree* star
43 Smile broadly
47 Newscast segment
49 The theater, for some
51 Mideast ruler
53 Himalayan land
55 Pub servings
56 City in Colombia
57 *Inside* __ (Gunther book)
58 Camp shelter
59 Chemical ending
60 Inc., in Ipswich
61 Anger
62 Paper Mate competitor

3 BORN YESTERDAY (1946)

"What's a peninsula?" "It's that new medicine."

ACROSS

1 Hardly anything, so to speak
6 Sonic bounce
10 Important people
14 *Ulysses* surname
15 Sketch
16 Scarlett's daughter in *Scarlett*
17 Lead role of the play
19 Withdraw gradually
20 Wool source
21 Dramatic device
22 Put on, as a play
26 *Rhinoceros* playwright
28 Dental work
29 Prince Harry's grandfather
31 Sightseeing trip
32 Business bigwig
33 British royal house
37 S&L conveniences
38 Quickness
40 Harris honorific
41 Fix, as a shoe
43 Poetic nighttime
44 Singer Horne
45 *Bonanza* setting
47 Biblical peak
48 Bumppo's nickname

51 *Applause* star
52 Neighborhoods
53 Domain
56 Mrs. David Bowie
57 Tycoon role in the play
62 Dolly's last name
63 Coup d'__
64 Intermission follower
65 *East of* __
66 *The Untouchables* memoirist
67 Exemplar of evil

DOWN

1 Bond rating
2 Inventor Whitney
3 Warner Books owner
4 Lon of Cambodia
5 Le Carré character
6 Norse epic
7 Study hard
8 Michener novel
9 Have the title to
10 Paul Verrall's employer in the play
11 Miscellanies
12 Bugs Bunny's voice
13 Sony competitor

18 Days of yore
21 "What's __ for me?"
22 Indian instrument
23 Government security
24 Reunion attendees
25 Author of the play
27 *Daily Planet* reporter
29 Princess perturber
30 Watered down, in a way
32 Mercury alternative
34 Sports stadium
35 Kidney-related
36 Pioneer's creation
39 Sri Lanka export
42 Wine sediment
46 Treat with carbon dioxide
47 Brazilian dances
48 __ Selassie
49 Carrying a weapon
50 Use a loom
51 Fogg emulator
54 Epochs
55 Lively group
57 Female turkey
58 Sarnoff's company
59 Mel of baseball
60 Jack Ryan org.
61 Reunion attendees

The role of 17 Across was originally
intended for Jean Arthur.

Judy
Holliday
was a last-
minute
replacement
during
out-of-
town
tryouts.

She learned her lines in only three days.

4 BUS STOP (1955)

"I understand everything I say, and secretly despise the way I say it."

ACROSS

1 Celery piece
6 Companies
11 Go bad
14 __ in Love
15 Son of Abraham
16 Pitcher's stat
17 Stood up
18 National bird
19 Command to a dog
20 Professor role in the play
22 Vietnamese holiday
23 Gratified
24 Pizzeria spice
26 *The Heart Is a Lonely Hunter* character
29 Actress Hedren
31 Flivver
32 *Arabian Nights* name
33 __ Webster (Twain frog)
34 Shortened wd. form
36 Salten book
38 Wander (about)
40 __ *on Bread* (cookbook)
43 Flower's beginning
45 Industrial containers
47 Society-page word
48 Actors' reps.
50 French school
52 School attended by James Bond
53 "I have no idea!"
55 Oaf
57 Storage container
58 Author of the play
63 Course for new immigrants: Abbr.
64 *Anthony Adverse* author
65 Bikini, for one
66 View
67 *Lost Horizon* transportation
68 Arthur Hailey novel
69 Foxlike
70 Sealy competitor
71 Field of battle

DOWN

1 Ill-gotten gains
2 Went quickly
3 Greek love god
4 *Gil Blas* author
5 Mournful sound
6 Tom Jones creator
7 Exeter exclamation
8 Ames Brothers tune
9 Tropical affliction
10 Act division
11 Setting for much of the play
12 Pacific Rim region
13 *The Rose* __
21 Statistical info
25 Comedian Kaplan
26 Boxer's punch
27 Harper Lee's home: Abbr.
28 Original cast member of the play
30 *Dialogues* author
33 "The __ is cast"
35 Air-gun ammo
37 Word on a Tony
39 *Don Quixote* character
41 '20s auto
42 "A __ of thieves"
44 *Oklahoma!* choreographer
46 Actor Lugosi
48 *The Sound of Music* character
49 Seuss' real surname
51 Wine area
52 Newspaper exec
54 One-for-one deal
56 Fred Astaire's birthplace
59 Mardi Gras follower
60 Make mention of
61 Secluded valley
62 Singer Fitzgerald

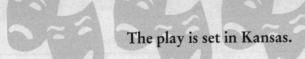

The play is set in Kansas.

28 Down originated the role portrayed by Marilyn Monroe in the film version.

Elaine Stritch originated the role of 11 Down owner Grace.

1	2	3	4	5		6	7	8	9	10		11	12	13
14						15						16		
17						18						19		
20					21						22			
			23				24			25				
26	27	28			29		30				31			
32				33					34	35				
36			37			38		39		40			41	42
		43			44		45		46			47		
48	49				50	51				52				
53				54				55		56				
57				58			59					60	61	62
63				64					65					
66				67				68					
69				70				71					

5 EDWARD ALBEE

First play: *The Zoo Story* (1959)

ACROSS

1 South Pacific island
5 *For __ the Bell Tolls*
9 Blazing
14 Just
15 What was left in Pandora's box
16 First-anniversary gift
17 Spiny houseplant
18 Impressionist
19 *Love __ the Ruins*
20 Albee play
22 Playbill listings
23 Addison's colleague
24 Chaps
25 Dramatis personae
29 Pats gently
33 Successful, as a play
37 Sharpen
38 Christmas season
39 Air-freshener targets
40 Forty winks
41 "The Outcasts of Poker Flat" author
42 Turkish money
43 Olympus boss
44 Pile up
45 Ten C-notes
46 Departs from the script
48 EPA calculation
50 Thomas More book
55 *Odyssey* creator
58 Albee play
61 Gladiator venue
62 Slightly
63 High schooler
64 Cooper character
65 Broadway version of 8½
66 *God's Little __*
67 Cinderella slipper material
68 Linda of *Jekyll & Hyde*
69 Hounds and hamsters

DOWN

1 Farm animals
2 Darkened
3 Unaccompanied
4 "Baloney!"
5 The *Pequod*, for one
6 Arizona Indian
7 Oil cartel
8 Insignificant
9 Quickly
10 Albee play
11 Wall St. debuts
12 Play based on *La Bohème*
13 Units of work
21 Opera voices
24 Ran into
26 Had possession of
27 Ryder rival
28 Coke alternative
30 Invisible emanation
31 Crunchy sandwiches
32 Bishops' domains
33 Texas tie
34 Valhalla VIP
35 Links warning
36 Albee play
41 Quickness
43 Make a sharp turn
47 *The __ Battle Book*
49 Beseeches
51 Readily available
52 Music selection
53 Unmoving
54 *__ of God* (Pielmeier play)
55 Put up a picture
56 Vocal
57 Prefix for physics
58 *The Producers* Tony winner
59 Footnote abbreviation
60 Trig function

6 THE CHERRY ORCHARD (1904)

"Dear and most respected bookcase! I welcome your existence."

ACROSS

1 Spy org.
4 German autos
8 Sir Walter Scott novel
14 Diner order
15 Show team spirit
16 Still green
17 Superlative suffix
18 Subtle atmosphere
19 Improperly obtained
20 Cherry orchard owner
22 Con-game participants
23 Memo
24 Mr. Coward
25 One more than *zwei*
28 Woody's son
30 CNN rival
34 Rap group
36 Emilia's husband
38 Fury
39 Paramedic: Abbr.
40 Author of the play
42 Scratched out
43 Japanese playwright
44 Existed
45 Far-off
47 __ Hare
49 Author Dinesen
51 Picnic spoilers
52 *And Still I* __
54 Colorings
56 Irving title character
59 Varya's suitor in the play
63 Remained steadfast
64 Some nest eggs
65 "Without further __ . . ."
66 Magic charm
67 Unimportant
68 San Diego attraction
69 Track officials
70 Poses a question
71 Antlered animal

DOWN

1 Trucker with a transmitter
2 *Casablanca* character
3 Envelope abbreviation
4 Word of approval
5 40 Across sported one
6 *The Miracle* __
7 Don't leave
8 __-Japanese War
9 Active
10 Uses a barbecue
11 Lunar valley
12 German car
13 Hankerings
21 Geraint's wife
24 One of the Joad boys
25 Reverie
26 Latin dance
27 Stage direction
29 Takes a shine to
31 *Six Crises* author
32 *The Sun Also Rises* character
33 Gives up
35 Guinness Book compilers' surname
37 Martin Cruz Smith novel
41 Pennsylvania port
46 *The Man in the Iron* __
48 Nursery furniture
50 Dotes on
53 Leopard feature
55 Simplifies
56 __ *Championship Season*
57 Prefix for "half"
58 Sad
59 South American capital
60 Lolita's last name
61 Graven image
62 Cozy spot

Varya is Madame 20 Across' stepdaughter.

20 Across' first name is Lyubov.

59 Across' first name is Yermolay.

The crossword grid:

1	2	3	■	4	5	6	7	■	8	9	10	11	12	13
14			■	15				■	16					
17			■	18				■	19					
20			21				■	22						
■	■	■	23				■	24				■	■	■
25	26	27		■	28		29		■	30		31	32	33
34			■	35		■	36		37		■	38		
39			■	40		41			■		42			
43			■	44			■	45		46				
47			48		■	49		50		■	51			
■	■	■	52		53	■	54		55		■	■	■
56	57	58				■	59				60	61	62
63				■	64				■	65			
66				■	67				■	68			
69				■	70				■	71			

7 THE CRUCIBLE (1953)

"I am innocent to a witch. I know not what a witch is."

ACROSS

1 *White __* (London novel)
5 Designer Gucci
9 Use finger paint
14 Four Corners state
15 Reclined
16 *Places in the __*
17 Something forbidden
18 It's n. of Chicago
19 Makes easier
20 Setting of the play
23 Commandments word
24 Ambulance driver, often: Abbr.
25 LXX times X
28 "Sweet are the __ of adversity"
31 Rise
36 In the country
38 Honest-to-goodness
40 "Summertime" is one
41 Accused witch in the play
44 *La Bohème* character
45 Oboist's need
46 Beginning
47 Act beginning
49 "The Gloomy __" (Inge)
51 Language suffix
52 Mach 2 flyer
54 Chicken part
56 Priggish preacher in the play
63 Minor Prophet
64 Turns bad
65 Sale condition
67 Benedict Arnold collaborator
68 Use the tub
69 Norse epic
70 Ed Koch book
71 *Born Free* beast
72 Harmony, for short

DOWN

1 Games partner
2 Molecule division
3 Barrie sheepdog
4 *Hamlet* spirit
5 Irving Berlin waltz
6 Not of the clergy
7 Cable-TV alternative
8 When expected
9 Ream component
10 Veal or venison
11 "It is the __, and Juliet . . ."
12 Trojan War instigator
13 ACLU concern
21 Football coach Don
22 Kemelman's rabbi
25 Apothecary weights
26 Third-degree, in math
27 Whodunit investigation
29 Perry's creator
30 Did darning
32 *Double Indemnity* author
33 Delete
34 French city
35 Esthetic sense
37 Not "fer"
39 Right-hand person
42 Like Joyce
43 Hermit
48 Old Testament queen
50 *The Call of the Wild* setting
53 Of few words
55 *The Tin Drum* author
56 __ *Lisa*
57 *Show Boat* captain
58 Poi source
59 Sweater material
60 Sch. auxiliaries
61 Brit's "Hey!"
62 Aries or Pisces
63 Improvisation session
66 Kangaroo pouch, e.g.

Arthur Miller wrote the play as a thinly
veiled attack on the McCarthy era.

It ran for
only 197
performances
in its
first
Broadway
run.

It ran nearly three times as long in its
first revival off-Broadway in 1958.

8 CYRANO DE BERGERAC (1897)

"How Fate loves a jest!"

ACROSS

1 London newspaper
6 Poise or diplomacy
11 "Be quiet!"
14 Video-game name
15 Expound on
16 Asian belief
17 With 63 Across, friend of Cyrano
19 Internet location, for short
20 Decide on
21 Frog feature
22 Type of housecat
24 Hosp. area
25 *Dombey and __*
26 Washington Irving character
28 *The Name Above the Title* autobiographer
30 Prepare for a bout
32 Circle dance
33 Doctors' org.
35 Very long time
37 *The Bridge of San Luis __*
38 Author of the play
42 Aberdeen assent
43 Fusses
44 Midmorning
45 Salon job

47 Miner's rocks
49 Fort Knox bar
53 Grisham novel
55 Author Rand
57 *The Yearling* character
58 Hale exile
59 Artist's medium
61 Notary need
62 Actor Wallach
63 See 17 Across
66 Dry, as wine
67 Ruhr city
68 Dumas swordsman
69 Former Air France plane
70 Poet Lizette
71 A question of location

DOWN

1 Ploy
2 Ulysses' home
3 Profit source
4 Buffalo's lake
5 Family member
6 O-Lan and Gunga Din
7 Orion's Belt component
8 Hemingway angler
9 Timetable abbr.
10 Saw parts

11 Ornery
12 Kept protected
13 Easter, for one
18 *__ for the Seesaw*
23 "Open wide!" response
25 Mead hangout
27 Wave top
29 Door buster
31 Analyze a sentence
34 Two-part conjunction
36 Virgil Thomson collaborator
38 Sneaker parts
39 Abandoned ship
40 Carroll character
41 Author Beattie
42 Relevance
46 Graduate deg.
48 Like brine
50 *Faust* author
51 Spellbinding speaker
52 *Honor Thy Father* author
54 __ sanctum
56 Designer monogram
60 Currier collaborator
61 *Abe Lincoln in Illinois* character
64 Compass reading
65 Statute

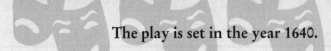

The play is set in the year 1640.

It had its
American
premiere
in New
York City
in 1898.

**38 Across was elected to the Académie
Française in 1901.**

9 DEATH OF A SALESMAN (1949)

"Pop, I'm a dime a dozen and so are you."

ACROSS

1 Colleen
5 Crop bundle
10 With 68 Across, Willy Loman portrayer in 1949
14 Part of the eye
15 Monopoly prop
16 Church area
17 Blackbird
18 Chew the scenery
19 Food plan
20 Willy Loman portrayer in 1999
23 "Me too!"
24 Expert
25 Scenery chewer
28 *Inherit the Wind* focus
32 Marx collaborator
34 Signed on
36 Chapters of history
37 Willy Loman portrayer in 1984
42 __ Hari
43 Little Lord Fauntleroy's first name
44 Proverbs preceder
47 Baseball activity
52 "Silence!"
53 Tread the boards
55 *Taming of the Shrew* setting
56 Willy Loman portrayer in 1975
60 *Two Years Before the Mast* author
63 Hester's daughter
64 Hawaiian city
65 Nasal appraisal
66 Wonderland cake words
67 Broadway actress Linda
68 See 10 Across
69 Heat source
70 Auction units

DOWN

1 One of the vertebrae
2 Loath
3 *Flash Gordon*, e.g.
4 Sandwich filler
5 Molt
6 *Harvest* __ (Tryon novel)
7 Orwell alma mater
8 Site of Vulcan's forge
9 Jason's quest
10 Tiger alternative
11 Prefix for center
12 Suffix for legal
13 Deep black
21 *Tender Is the* __
22 Female lobster
25 Mrs. Zeus
26 __ Jay Lerner
27 Submissions to eds.
29 Second-sequel indicator
30 Sarah __ Jewett
31 Gandhi colleague
33 Ruby, for instance
35 College quarters
37 "__ away all!"
38 Zion National Park locale
39 *On the Road* character
40 Beau Brummell
41 Acrobatic stunts
42 GI police
45 Ginnie __
46 "Monkey Trial" defendant
48 Author Carson
49 Preston/Martin musical
50 Certain small seed
51 Florida footballers
54 Unexpected pleasure
56 Apparel
57 *Barbarians at the* __
58 Writer Bombeck
59 Red Skelton character
60 One of the Dwarfs
61 Ruckus
62 __ Hill (San Francisco district)

10 DAVID MAMET

First play: 43 Across (1970)

ACROSS

1 Under the weather
5 First name in Western fiction
9 Nautical direction
14 Actor Morales
15 Perry victory site
16 Hidden supply
17 Mamet play
20 Poetic preposition
21 Half of CCVI
22 Charges
23 British prison
25 Dog's warning
26 Blonde shade
27 Mamet play
32 Sugar source
35 Part of QED
36 *The Time Machine* race
37 *The Jetsons* kid
38 Author Deighton
39 Fr. misses
40 State with confidence
41 Actress Merrill
42 Leavening agent
43 See blurb at top
45 Employee ID, often
46 Fiscal periods: Abbr.
47 *Leave It to Beaver* surname
51 *The Jungle Book* character
55 *The Plains of Passage* author
56 German pronoun
57 Mamet play
60 *Broadway Bound* actress
61 Doctor's imperative
62 Gusto
63 Whom Sherlock called "the woman"
64 Phnom __
65 Italian princely name

DOWN

1 __ *Keys to Baldpate*
2 French river
3 Cavalier poet
4 Kipling title character
5 *Babbitt* setting
6 *Lost in Yonkers* kid
7 Unless: Lat.
8 "A mouse!"
9 Equity members
10 Walking speed
11 Pulitzer contemporary
12 Ostrichlike bird
13 Diagnostic procedure
18 *Juno and the Paycock* writer
19 Marsh dweller
24 *Goldfinger* character
25 African nation
27 E.C. Bentley detective
28 Western capital
29 __ breve
30 Misfortunes
31 "To do" sheet
32 Ground grain
33 Thomas __ Edison
34 Nursery school, for short
35 Inventor Howe
39 "Song of __" (Whitman work)
41 Column order
44 Column credit
45 Chan or Spade
47 Castro, for one
48 Perfume holders
49 Showy display
50 French river
51 Where Timbuktu is
52 "A Jug of Wine" poet
53 "__ Only Just Begun"
54 Cheshire Cat expression
55 Part of A.M.
58 African snake
59 Service charge

His pre-literary career included jobs as a cab driver and at a real estate agency.

He won a Pulitzer Prize for *Glengarry Glen Ross.*

His screenplays include *Wag the Dog* and *Hannibal.*

11 DEATHTRAP (1978)

"Sound construction, good dialogue, laughs in the right places. Highly commercial."

ACROSS

1 Juvenile ammo
4 African antelopes
8 News sources of yore
14 Southwestern creek
15 *Letting Go* author
16 *Hiroshima* author
17 Media conglomerate
18 Water, to Juan
19 Arthurian paradise
20 "Big red dog" of kiddie lit
22 __ Aviv
23 "Cut that out!"
24 Penpoint
26 Harris storyteller
30 Titania's spouse
32 Uplift
34 Loch monster, affectionately
37 Moslem cleric
38 *Paradise Lost* character
42 Psychic role in the play
43 *M*A*S*H* drink
44 Doozy
45 Most uncommon
47 Depicts on stage
49 Spillane sleuth
54 Elevator alternative
55 Sea plea
58 Nancy Drew series surname
59 OSS successor
61 *What Price Glory?* author
63 Waterfall phenomenon
66 Whistle sound
67 Tint
68 *The Lion in Winter* star
69 Art Deco artist
70 Fabergé collectible
71 Persian king
72 Spotted
73 Haggard novel

DOWN

1 *The Graduate* star of 2002
2 Underwater research station
3 Rich in NaCl
4 *E Is for Evidence* author
5 NASA negative
6 Direction reversal
7 *A __ of Difference* (Drury novel)
8 Informal conversation
9 Midnight rider of poems
10 Author of the play
11 Subj. for new citizens
12 Antique car
13 Thesaurus entry: Abbr.
21 Evergreen
25 Brown shade
27 "Life is a banquet" lady
28 See 40 Down
29 Prefix for solid
31 Statesman of India
33 Canine controller
35 Theater units
36 Kind of camera: Abbr.
38 "So sorry!"
39 Conduit
40 With 28 Down, Western ski resort
41 Broadway theater where the play opened
46 Director's directive
48 Maryland's state bird
50 Body of *eau*
51 Openwork fabrics
52 "No more!"
53 Go back on a deal
56 *Bellefleur* author
57 Night noise
60 Fills with reverence
62 Spoil, perhaps, with "on"
63 Chi baseballers
64 Sport __ (car category)
65 Common conjunction

The veteran playwright in the play is Sidney Bruhl.

His most successful play is *The Murder Game.*

42 Across' last name is ten Dorp.

1	2	3		4	5	6	7		8	9	10	11	12	13
14				15					16					
17				18					19					
20			21						22					
23					24		25		26		27	28	29	
30				31			32	33						
			34		35	36				37				
38	39	40	41		42					43				
44					45				46					
47			48					49		50	51	52	53	
54					55	56	57		58					
			59		60		61		62					
63	64	65					66				67			
68							69				70			
71							72				73			

12 THE EMPEROR JONES (1920)

"I got brains and I uses 'em quick. Dat ain't luck."

ACROSS

1 *GoodFellas* actor
6 *1776* nickname
9 Brinker footwear
14 Painter's pigment
15 Oath affirmation
16 Malcolm X biographer
17 Madrid museum
18 __ *Miz*
19 Pear alternative
20 Author of the play
23 Mae West play
24 *Musical __* (Rodgers autobiography)
28 Where Jones escapes to
34 St. Petersburg's river
35 Overcast
36 Puts to work
38 Four times CCLI
39 *Superfudge* author
40 Western Hemisphere alliance
41 Complaining sound
43 __ Lingus
44 *Elle et lui* author
46 *Taming of the Shrew* character
47 Actress Chase
49 Setting of the play
51 Must
53 Kander collaborator
54 The only thing Jones believes can hurt him
61 __ *Knot* (Fugard play)
64 Annoy
65 Bestseller by 16 Across
66 Ballet rail
67 Compass pt.
68 GATT successor
69 Ear cleaners
70 Scale note
71 Go on stage

DOWN

1 "An Essay on Man" author
2 Hosiery shade
3 Carpet type
4 Relinquish
5 *Old __* (Holmes poem subject)
6 __ *Blues* (Simon play)
7 Churchill successor
8 Cyrano's prominent feature
9 Commandment word
10 Rosten title character
11 Matterhorn, for one
12 Business card abbr.
13 Surveil
21 Counting-out starter
22 "It's clear now!"
25 Zodiac sign
26 Show clearly
27 Word-processor function
28 *87th Precinct* series author
29 Mutated gene
30 *Fantasy Island* host
31 Rum __ Tugger
32 Campus areas
33 Battleship letters
37 *Songs Before Sunrise* poet
40 *A Chorus Line* finale
42 Formerly owned
45 Naval offense: Abbr.
46 Lettuce variety
48 Collect on a surface
50 *Working* author
52 *The Prince of __*
55 Contends
56 Cube man Rubik
57 Cash advance
58 Artist's residence, perhaps
59 Diminutive suffix
60 Romanov ruler
61 Projectile pellets
62 Scott Turow genre
63 "Are you a man __ mouse?"

The title character's first name is Brutus.

He is a convict and former Pullman car attendant.

He is assisted in his schemes by British trader Henry Smithers.

13 FENCES (1985)

"Life don't owe you nothing. You owe it to yourself."

ACROSS

1 *The Immigrants* author
5 Erupt
9 Happy or Grumpy
14 __ podrida
15 Ripped
16 Poetic feet
17 Sad
18 *Casablanca* heroine
19 Done in
20 28 Across drives one in the play
23 South American capital
24 Unleashed
28 Main character of the play
33 __ of the above
34 Meet again, as alumni
35 Epoch
36 Actress Thompson
37 Legal counsel: Abbr.
38 More in need of cleaning
42 French apéritif
43 Russian river
45 New Deal org.
46 Make __ in (achieve some progress)
48 Tiny bit
49 Setting of the play
52 *Cocoon* Oscar winner
54 Kemo __
55 Author of the play
61 *The Gathering* __ (Churchill book)
64 Skin feature
65 *Leave __ Me* (Porter musical)
66 *Pal Joey* playwright
67 Persian poet
68 Global defense grp.
69 Tempter of Odysseus
70 Siestas
71 Understand, à la Heinlein

DOWN

1 Passepartout's boss
2 __ breve
3 Speak indistinctly
4 *tom thumb* star
5 Mark of shame
6 Medieval weapon
7 Prefix for while
8 Be dressed in
9 '70s music style
10 Small roles
11 *I __ Camera*
12 Baseball stat
13 Half a sawbuck
21 Hoped (to)
22 Forearm bones
25 Heavy rain
26 Surprise __
27 Shortage
28 Shock to the system
29 Lower the hedges again
30 Surpassed at a buffet
31 Attack
32 "It must be him, __ shall die"
39 Open, in a way
40 __ Lanka
41 David Small, e.g.
44 *A Perfect Spy* author
47 *Scaramouche* activity
50 Woman's shoe feature
51 Carpenters, often
53 *The __ Comedy* (Saroyan book)
56 Second word of "The Raven"
57 *Brave New World* drug
58 Rigel or Sirius
59 Anne Frank's father
60 Sheltered spot
61 Distress signal
62 Summer weather letters
63 Crew-team implement

The Broadway role of 28 Across was
originated by James Earl Jones.

The play
won a
Tony
Award, a
Pulitzer
Prize and
a New
York
Drama
Critics
Circle
Award.

28 Across' brother Gabe believes he is
the archangel Gabriel.

"Pretty girls are a trap, a pretty trap, and men expect them to be."

ACROSS

1 Afternoon TV fare
6 *The King and I* setting
10 Random House cofounder
14 Sleep disorder
15 Jason's vessel
16 Palo __, CA
17 What 63 Across calls a suitor
20 Entraps
21 Mouse spotter's sounds
22 Start of a JFK quote
23 *Garden of Earthly Delights* painter
25 Has an evening meal
27 Investor's risk, for short
29 A U.S. alliance
31 Foreign correspondent of a sort
35 Amble
36 Circus setting
38 *Sunset Boulevard* main character
39 Part of NATO
40 Setting of the play
42 Dictionary abbr.
43 Melanie, to Pittypat
45 Author Ambler
46 Fr. ladies
47 Sartre work
49 Language suffix
50 Prefix for nautical
51 Boris Godunov, for one
53 Chicago-based film reviewer
55 *The __ in the Hat*
58 British prep school
60 Gibson of tennis
63 Main character of the play
66 Grain storehouse
67 Horse hair
68 Occupied
69 Sounds of disapproval
70 Don Juan's mother
71 Wine bouquets

DOWN

1 Gets tired
2 Receiving customers
3 Poe poem
4 '70s fad gift
5 Willy Loman's line
6 Dodsworth's first name
7 *Dies __*
8 Actress Moorehead
9 Full-size model
10 Presidential nickname
11 Singer Fitzgerald
12 AAA suggestions
13 Dinnerware piece
18 Chaperon
19 Poplar relatives
24 __ Selassie
26 __-Cone
27 Proust title character
28 Barbecue place
30 Say "SKNXX-X!"
32 Aeschylus title character
33 *Forever __*
34 Cow catcher
37 External appearance
40 Appropriated
41 Sprain application
44 190, in old Rome
46 Singer with a role in *The Godfather*
48 Japanese mat
52 *Laugh-In* cohost
54 Like Rumpelstiltskin
55 Playbill listing
56 *The Rachel Papers* author
57 Gab
59 Certain stitch's saving
61 Otherwise
62 Fruit drinks
64 Turndowns
65 Pince-__ glasses

Tennessee Williams described this semi-autobiographical work as a "memory play."

He originally wrote the play as a film script while employed at MGM.

1	2	3	4	5		6	7	8	9		10	11	12	13
14						15					16			
17					18				19					
20							21					22			
		23				24		25			26			
27	28				29		30		31			32	33	34
35					36			37		38				
39				40					41			42		
43			44			45					46			
47					48		49				50			
		51			52		53		54					
55	56	57		58			59		60				61	62
63				64					65					
66					67					68				
69					70					71				

The play's title refers to 63 Across' daughter's collection of animals.

15 ARTHUR MILLER

First play: *The Man Who Had All the Luck* (1944)

ACROSS

1 Austen novel
5 Olivier, for one
9 Secret plot
14 Transact business
15 Highly rated
16 *Foreign Affairs* author
17 Doctor's prescription
18 Karma
19 Stage whisper
20 With 58 Across, Miller play
22 Guide the ride
23 Madden
24 When spr. starts
25 Civil War initials
28 *The Shining* message
31 Envelope letters
35 Quickness
37 Tempest __ teapot
38 Pinocchio's undoing
39 Miller play
43 Broadway light
44 Dickens pseudonym
45 "The Old __ Bucket"
46 Overly theatrical
47 "Thanatopsis" poet
50 Wall St. overseer
51 Capone et al.
53 Five title characters of a
   musical

55 String quartet
   instrument
58 See 20 Across
63 Radio-studio sign
64 Original cast member of
   Arsenic and Old Lace
65 *Star Trek* captain
66 Federico García __
67 Anne Nichols hero
68 Cleveland's lake
69 Friend of Elizabeth I
70 Oustee of 1917
71 Theater crew's
   constructions

DOWN

1 Icelandic poem
2 Griffin of TV
3 Hawaiian island
4 *Tattered Tom* author
5 Confound
6 Laughed heartily
7 *Long Day's Journey __
   Night*
8 Abound
9 Envelope attachment
10 *The Thorn Birds* setting
11 Party cheese
12 Man Friday
13 Impolite look

21 Woodward's biography of
   John Belushi
24 Latin 101 verb
25 Pearl Buck's childhood
   home
26 More sensible
27 *My Fair Lady* setting
29 Posh
30 *The Faerie Queene*
   character
32 Watch sounds
33 Giggle sound
34 '90s rock group
36 Albee play
40 Recedes
41 "__ iron bars a cage"
42 Member of the electorate
48 Fielding novel
49 "Whether 'tis __ in the
   mind . . ."
52 Seuss conservationist
54 Fagin associate
55 King of rhyme
56 Son of Seth
57 *I Remember Mama* papa
58 One of those things
59 Central locations
60 Calamitous
61 Courage
62 Supplements, with "out"

His first literary success was his novel,
Focus, published in 1945.

1	2	3	4	■	5	6	7	8	■	9	10	11	12	13
14				■	15				■	16				
17				■	18				■	19				
20			21						■	22				

He wrote
the
screenplay
of *The
Misfits* for
his wife,
Marilyn
Monroe.

His autobiography, *Timebends*, was
published in 1987.

16 GLENGARRY GLEN ROSS (1984)

"First prize is a Cadillac Eldorado . . . . Second prize is a set of steak knives.
Third prize is you're fired."

ACROSS

1 Sour-tasting
6 Moore of *Purlie*
11 Cal. page
14 *West Side Story* heroine
15 Tony, for instance
16 Actress Gardner
17 Peter __ Tchaikovsky
18 Icy cold
19 Vet patient
20 Character in the play
22 Do-it-yourselfer's buy
23 Extinct bird
24 Mrs. Leopold Bloom
26 Mr. Melville
30 Shelley's middle name
33 States confidently
34 Oats or barley
35 *Barnaby Rudge* character
38 Wife of Jacob
39 *My Friend Flicka* author
40 Ariz. neighbor
41 *You __ Live Twice*
42 Yarn unit
43 Penned
44 Playwright Rostand
46 British economist
47 *Dames __* (off-Broadway musical)
49 That guy's

50 *The A-Team* star
51 Original portrayer of 20 Across
59 Soup veggie
60 Talk-show tycoon
61 Scarlett's mother
62 Allow
63 Sicilian peak
64 Repaired, in a way
65 Compass pt.
66 *Final __* (Houseman memoir)
67 *My Life and Fortunes* author

DOWN

1 Mideast ruler
2 City in Colombia
3 Knight who wrote *Lassie, Come Home*
4 *Rabbit Is __*
5 Popular cruise spot
6 A Gabor sister
7 Water pitcher
8 French composer
9 Cup top
10 Hull House cofounder
11 Star of the film version of the play
12 Be of use

13 *The Pathfinder* hero
21 Director Howard
25 "The Ransom of Red Chief" author
26 Heavenly headgear
27 Level
28 20 Across' business
29 Literary alter ego
30 *Destry Rides Again* author
31 Andrew's dukedom
32 Fitness center
34 Honolulu-based sleuth
36 Parcel (out)
37 Geometric reference lines
39 Taunting cry
43 Jay Gatsby's home
45 Steinbeck character
46 Relatives
47 More than enough
48 Kilmer poem
49 Laughing sounds
52 Letters on a phone
53 Russian-born artist
54 *Dead __ Walk* (McMurtry novel)
55 *Glamour* rival
56 Surfeit
57 Nair alternative
58 Rooney of *60 Minutes*

The title refers to 28 Down developments being sold in the play.

Other stars in the original cast included Robert Prosky and J.T. Walsh.

17 HAMLET (1601)

"Brevity is the soul of wit."

ACROSS

1 Beef cut
5 Tenure of office
9 Literary genre
14 Polynesian Cultural Center locale
15 Part of the eye
16 Brother of Moses
17 Hamlet's title
20 Go bad
21 Capital of Ukraine
22 Item for Bulfinch
23 Adorable
25 Evergreen tree
27 __-Lytton
30 Hamlet's stepfather
34 "A Chapter on Ears" byline
35 "No man is an __"
37 Single-helix molecule
38 Prefix for mural
40 *The __ Drum* (Grass book)
41 Paperless messages
43 Burns' refusal
44 Awkward
47 Pot starter
48 Hamlet's mother
50 Oscar winner as Disraeli
52 Counting-rhyme starter
53 Oil cartel
54 Custardy dessert
57 Burn slightly
59 Largest artery
63 Polonius' title
66 "Farewell!"
67 Half of CVI
68 Talking horse of TV
69 Steinbeck short story, with "The"
70 "Shall we?" response
71 Gen-__ (Baby Boomers' kids)

DOWN

1 Wambaugh characters
2 *The Grass __* (Capote book)
3 Where Winesburg is
4 Julius Caesar book subject
5 Calendar abbreviation
6 Call forth
7 Mortgage holder's option, for short
8 Prepared
9 Cupid's first name
10 Hit head-on
11 Like __ of sunshine
12 Humorist Sahl
13 Egyptian cross
18 Cigar ash, for Sherlock
19 French spa
24 Numerical prefix
26 *__ Descending a Staircase*
27 Existence
28 Arm bones
29 Soda-bottle size
30 Surroundings, to a poet
31 Teheran resident
32 Textbook divisions
33 Corporate division
36 High-school period
39 Square-mile fraction
42 Alex Haley subject
45 Cafeteria offering
46 Big mouth
49 *__ Is the Night*
51 Bring up
53 Sphere of influence
54 Commotion
55 Mine strike
56 Sills solo
58 Grenoble girlfriend
60 Nearly unobtainable
61 Theater level
62 "No ifs, __, or buts!"
64 __-de-sac
65 *__ for Evidence*

The "play within a play" is *The Murder of Gonzago.*

1	2	3	4		5	6	7	8		9	10	11	12	13
14					15					16				
17				18				19						
20						21				22				
			23		24			25	26					
27	28	29					30				31	32	33	
34					35	36				37				
38				39		40			41	42				
43				44	45			46		47				
48			49				50	51						
			52			53								
54	55	56			57		58		59		60	61	62	
63				64			65							
66					67			68						
69					70			71						

At 3,933 lines, this is the longest of Shakespeare's plays.

The title character has 1,569 lines, more than any other Shakespearean character.

"I've wrestled with reality for 35 years, and I'm happy to say I finally won out over it."

ACROSS

1 Property crime
6 *Burr* author
11 Scratch up
14 __ voce
15 From the beginning: Lat.
16 Physicians' org.
17 Casino area
18 Insignificant
19 Box-score column heading
20 Main character of the play
22 Yang's partner
23 Be inconsistent
24 Spurns
26 Unskilled worker
29 Well-heeled
30 Bank conveniences: Abbr.
34 Thailand neighbor
36 Castle protectors
39 Auto racer A.J.
40 Raffles, for one
42 Exam for some coll. seniors
43 Ancient strings
45 Library patron
46 Counting-out starter
47 "Adieu!"
49 Author Ludwig
51 Most sedate
54 Vergil epic hero
59 Had a snack
60 What the title character is
63 Family member
64 Parcel out
65 Great-grandmother of David
66 Actress Thurman
67 Nostalgia clothing style
68 Specialty fisherman
69 Pilot's heading: Abbr.
70 Boxer Mike
71 Helps with the dishes

DOWN

1 Stubborn beasts
2 Actress Esther
3 *Dred* author
4 Preminger et al.
5 "It didn't work!"
6 Theda Bara screen persona
7 Footnote abbr.
8 Blood-bank visitor
9 One giving testimony
10 Conrad novel
11 Author of the play
12 Sphere of influence
13 Comes down hard
21 Resided
25 French school
27 *From Here to Eternity* setting
28 Cacophony
30 CIO's merger partner
31 Top or train
32 Niece of 20 Across
33 "__ Heat" (*Pajama Game* tune)
35 Appear to be
37 *The Hundred Secret Senses* author
38 Piggery
41 Tuck, for one
44 Portrayer of 20 Across in the film version
48 Twelve Oaks resident
50 Had a tendency
51 *The Stranger* writer
52 Energy source
53 Pinball infractions
55 Pro cager
56 *Christ Stopped at __*
57 Evangelist Macpherson
58 Swizzles
61 Picador's opponent
62 Town on the Thames

Harvey is a pooka, an invisible 60
Across seen only by 20 Across.

11 Down
based the
title
character
on Celtic
folk tales
she heard
as a child.

The original production was directed by
Antoinette Perry, for whom the Tony
Award is named.

19 HEDDA GABLER (1891)

"I've the most extraordinary longing to say 'Bloody hell!'"

ACROSS

1 Ethereal instrument
5 Savory jelly
10 Word form for "foreigner"
14 Jai __
15 Strauss specialty
16 On the summit
17 *The Magic Mountain* author
18 Playing marble
19 Archibald of basketball
20 Adjective for the title character
23 Like 1% milk
26 Coal carrier
27 Emulate Bing
28 Rightful
31 Hearing-related
35 Author of the play
38 Organic-compound suffix
39 *Der __* (Adenauer)
40 Nonmetric writing
41 Actress Swenson
42 Prefix for metric
43 Old school friend of the title character
45 "The Wizard of __ Park"
47 ACLU concern
48 Author Calvino
49 Greek letter

51 Legendary British isle
52 Husband of the title character
58 Imitative sort
59 Pulsate
60 Wife of __ (*Canterbury Tales* character)
64 Decrease
65 Wonderland cake phrase
66 Word on every U.S. coin
67 Plumlike fruit
68 Gloomy, in poetry
69 Brings up the rear

DOWN

1 *Green Eggs and __*
2 Fla. neighbor
3 Was a candidate
4 See 63 Down
5 Hang around for
6 Loses energy
7 City map
8 "Tell __ the Marines!"
9 Capek, e.g.
10 Coleridge locale
11 Coup d'__
12 Reply to the Little Red Hen
13 Vienna-based org.
21 Princess of India

22 Colorful horse
23 *Fiddler on the Roof* toast
24 Threat ender
25 Chinese dumpling
28 More grave
29 WWII sub
30 Road curves
32 Apartment, often
33 Heavenly being, in Bologna
34 Show the way
36 Autobahn speed measure: Abbr.
37 Elongated fish
41 City on two continents
43 Carryall
44 __ *Zapata!*
46 Stowe meanie
50 Paid up
51 Winsor title character
52 Benchley bestseller
53 Whitish gemstone
54 *Anything Goes* character
55 "__ she blows!"
56 Romain de Tirtoff alias
57 Fictional painkilling pill
61 Santa __, CA
62 Harbor craft
63 With 4 Down, Gilbert and Sullivan work

Nearly the entire play takes place in the title character's living room.

As the play begins, Hedda and 52 Across have just returned from a six-month honeymoon.

52 Across was raised by his Aunt Julle.

First play: *Bound East for Cardiff* (1916)

ACROSS

1 Ebenezer's partner
6 Army vehicle
10 Twist's request
14 Can't stand
15 Basilica section
16 "Beware the __ of March"
17 Isabella, for one
18 Actor Brad
19 Stool or settee
20 O'Neill play
23 Mornings, for short
26 Kipling character
27 Author __ Leonard
28 Chocolate confection
30 *An American Tragedy* character
32 Organic compound
33 One more than *dos*
35 Foreheads
39 O'Neill play
42 Euripides play
43 Assistant
44 *Damn Yankees* temptress
45 Penney competitor
47 Author Foote
49 Stretched one's neck
52 Trilogy containing *The Big Money*
53 Scottish assents
54 O'Neill play
58 Slanted line, in math: Abbr.
59 Male deer
60 *Same Time, Next Year* author
64 *Hedwig and the Angry __*
65 Compulsion
66 Seuss title character
67 Enthusiasm
68 Ase's son
69 *I Hated, Hated, Hated This Movie* author

DOWN

1 *The Bell __* (Plath book)
2 Playwright Burrows
3 Greek letter
4 O'Neill's daughter
5 *Streetcar* original cast member
6 *Shogun* setting
7 Like most Michener novels
8 Riga resident
9 Sea bird
10 Christie character
11 "__ the West Wind"
12 Broadcast again
13 Lauder of makeup
21 Beethoven's last symphony
22 Exclamation of amazement
23 Nautical direction
24 Street scam
25 Hair net
29 Wambaugh novel, with *The*
30 Suit
31 Cornerstone letters
34 *The __ of the Greasepaint . . .*
36 Alley Oop's wife
37 Robert Young TV role
38 Collar inserts
40 Transport for Lawrence
41 *Steppenwolf* author
46 Makes sense
48 Botheration
49 Port of Spain
50 *Watch on the __*
51 High-tech defense plane
52 Madison's roommate
55 To be, to Marie
56 *A __ to Live*
57 Unkempt one
61 "All the Things You __"
62 Patriotic org.
63 Business-card abbr.

His middle name was Gladstone.

He won the Nobel Prize for Literature in 1936.

His first full-length Broadway play was *Beyond the Horizon* in 1920.

21 I REMEMBER MAMA (1944)

"I remember Mama, with her very secret bank account, and a wide-open heart for other people's troubles."

ACROSS

1 Joyce Carol Oates book
5 Bunch of bees
10 Orchard element
14 *Come Back, Little Sheba* character
15 Desert stopovers
16 Bar mitzvah dance
17 __ *fan tutte*
18 Shouted out
19 Biblical twin
20 Author of the book that was the source of the play
23 Top bond rating
24 Bishop's domain
25 One of Mama's daughters
31 Reynolds competitor
35 Part of a bray
36 Macho guys
37 Eloise's home
38 Moslem title
40 Holds, as a theater
42 *The Lion King* villain
43 Actor Williamson
45 Mr. T TV series, with *The*
47 Early afternoon
48 Nervous
49 Mama, by birth
51 __-Cat (winter vehicle)
53 African beast
54 Author of the play
61 __ colada
62 Director Kurosawa
63 Study of sines
65 *One Flew __ the Cuckoo's Nest*
66 Performer's concern
67 Fictional Woodhouse
68 *The Shoes of the Fisherman* author
69 Hang-ups
70 Football cheers

DOWN

1 Close attention, for short
2 Barrie villain
3 Adamson subject
4 Rum drink
5 Greek philosopher
6 Suspicious
7 *Veeck __ Wreck* (baseball book)
8 Navigation hazard
9 Windows ancestor
10 Poe poem
11 *Gypsy* mother
12 Memorable periods
13 French water
21 Corned-beef concoction
22 Harvest
25 *The Good Earth* setting
26 Trap
27 Do a double take
28 "In other words . . ."
29 Slangy approval
30 __ *Whining* (Fran Drescher book)
32 Desert flora
33 Japanese-born conductor
34 *Silas Marner* character
39 *My Fair Lady* director on Broadway
41 Florida flora
44 Ms. Fontanne
46 Software options list
50 Rain diverter
52 Squashed circles
54 Baloney
55 Unspecified people
56 Similar
57 Ship of 1492
58 Bit of sediment
59 "Cope Book" aunt
60 Fictional rats' home
61 Sound of a punch
64 Argon or neon

20 Across' book is *Mama's Bank Account.*

The play was produced by Rodgers and Hammerstein.

A very young Marlon Brando made his Broadway debut playing Nels in the original cast.

22 THE ICEMAN COMETH (1946)

"Well, well! The Grandstand Foolosopher speaks!"

ACROSS

1 Golf-club part
6 Letters on fine brandy
10 Toe the line
14 Synagogue scroll
15 *The Sultan of __* (Ade book)
16 European capital, to natives
17 Conductor Previn
18 Rap star
19 *The Winds of War* author
20 Setting of the play
23 "To __ is human"
24 Actor Chaney
25 Neutron star
29 *I'm Not Rappaport* star
32 Mickey Mouse's dog
33 __ *Mater* (hymn)
36 Brit. flyers
38 Poetic adverb
39 Salesman in the play
43 Brain scan: Abbr.
44 Biblical land
45 High spirits
46 Mideast rulers
49 Author Westlake
51 Former Madrid money
53 WWW locale
54 Lamb sound

57 Portrayer of 39 Across in a 1956 revival
61 *The Rains __*
64 Some nest eggs
65 Pen name
66 Composer/author Wilder
67 Tropical fruit
68 Mooch
69 Broadway premiere of 1996
70 Plumbing fittings
71 Strike-zone border

DOWN

1 Vacant look
2 Obie, for instance
3 Zeal
4 *Animal __*
5 Trojan War epic
6 Churchillian gestures
7 Those kind of
8 Vegetable spread
9 Build
10 Author of 4 Down
11 *To Kill a Mockingbird* character
12 Flightless bird
13 Gab
21 *The Borrowers* author

22 Have an evening meal
26 *Guys and Dolls* tune
27 Eroded
28 Actor Cox
29 Network owned by AOL
30 Statement of belief
31 Defiant exclamation
33 Highly inclined
34 Essay
35 Auspices
37 Barber of opera
40 Mr. Serling
41 Auditioner's hope
42 Barnyard baby
47 Turn down
48 RR stop
50 Sips slowly, as a drink
52 Remark to the audience
54 She may face a judge
55 "Haste makes waste," for one
56 Beasts of burden
58 Type of exam
59 Countrywide: Abbr.
60 Milne's first name
61 Wheels
62 Tabard Inn serving
63 "I Hate __" (Porter tune)

The play is set in 1912 in New York City.

This was
the first
off-Broadway
revival to run
over 500
performances.

The 1956 revival cast also included
Peter Falk.

23 INHERIT THE WIND (1955)

"If the devil sends its Goliath into battle, it magnifies our cause."

ACROSS

1 Throat-culture finding
6 "That's awful!"
10 Indian melody
14 Battleground
15 Felipe of baseball
16 Wordsworth works
17 Knife name
18 Cajole
19 Money-making operation
20 Mess up
21 Tennessee setting of the play
23 Dr.-to-be's exam
25 Pencil end
26 *The African Queen* character
29 Louisiana inlet
31 Ghost's sound
32 "The Man Without a Country" character
34 Alternatively
38 Hornbeck's newspaper in the play
42 Worship from __
43 Showed deference
44 XIII quadrupled
45 *Hellzapoppin'* star
48 *High Button Shoes* director
50 Pale violet
53 *Black Mesa* author
54 Subject of the play
57 *Cagney & Lacey* actress
61 Boy: Sp.
62 __-European
63 Limber
64 Hoof sound
65 Free-for-all
66 Fund, as a scholarship
67 Racer of fable
68 French 101 verb
69 Thumbs-up votes

DOWN

1 Loses tension
2 Safari or cruise
3 Betting setting
4 Pulver, for one
5 Original cast member of the play
6 America's Cup entrant
7 Morlocks' prey
8 Fossil fuel
9 *Point Counter Point* author
10 *The Joy of Cooking* author
11 Lone Ranger's farewell
12 Sci-fi or romance
13 First American millionaire
22 Theater sign
24 Place for protons
26 *Mamma Mia!* songs source
27 Idle
28 Entertainer Falana
29 Bulwer-Lytton's title
30 From square one
33 Earring site
35 Composer Schifrin
36 Narrow cut
37 Do play doctoring, perhaps
39 *Phineas Finn* author
40 Learn (about)
41 Original cast member of the play
46 Brooklyn coll.
47 "What closes on Saturday night"
49 Author credit
50 *Shakespeare in Love* Oscar winner
51 Region of Spain
52 Pay tribute to
53 $1,000
55 "What's __ for me?"
56 Bouquet
58 Transportation stats.
59 Mother Goose residence
60 Assembles a shirt

The play was written by Jerome Lawrence and Robert E. Lee.

Tony Randall originated the role of reporter E.K. Hornbeck.

Hornbeck's character was based on H.L. Mencken.

ACROSS

1 Track event
5 Till compartment
9 OR imperative
13 Literary language of India
14 __ *Troll* (Heine book)
15 Jazz great Fountain
16 *Drums __ the Mohawk*
17 "Wonderful" vehicle in a Holmes poem
18 Silver State school: Abbr.
19 With 21 Across, coauthor of the play
21 See 19 Across
23 Spruce relatives
25 Serpent suffix
26 Compass pt.
27 Original cast member of the play
32 Yankee or Angel
33 __-jongg
34 "__ a Symphony" (Supremes tune)
38 Spill the beans
39 Key word in a Stone novel title
42 Oil giant's former name
43 *The Crucible* setting
45 __-TURN (highway sign)
46 Almanac features
47 Coauthor of the play
51 Belgian resort
54 Highway sign
55 Scored 100 on
56 With 58 Across, where the family home is
58 See 56 Across
62 Object of worship
63 Part of ABM
66 "__ my case!"
67 Istanbul resident
68 Inert gas
69 Plan stallers
70 Kid-lit skater
71 School founded by Henry VI
72 Are: Sp.

DOWN

1 *Catch-22* character
2 "Oh, Wilderness were Paradise __!"
3 *Saratoga Trunk* author
4 Fertile Crescent river
5 A U.S. alliance
6 To the __ degree
7 And others, in old Rome
8 Adage
9 Tater
10 Grammarian's concern
11 __ *Shrugged*
12 Memorable Mostel Broadway role
13 "That's what *you* think!"
20 Theater fare
22 Radar's soft drink
24 Booty
27 Slot inserts
28 Singer Fitzgerald
29 Factual
30 River of France
31 LeRoi Jones-edited anthology
35 Son of Isaac
36 Poisonous snakes
37 *Fences* character
40 Piano practice piece
41 Southwestern plant
44 Tousle
48 Mercury Theatre regular
49 Shakespearean form
50 Alter, as a libretto
51 *A Tree Grows in Brooklyn* author
52 *Kiss Me, Kate* setting
53 Decorate
57 Kinds
59 Well-ordered
60 Links rules org.
61 UFO pilots
64 Excessively
65 Quaint hotel

19 Across portrayed the title character in the original cast.

It is the longest-running non-musical Broadway play.

Alfred Lunt and Lynn Fontanne were the first choices to play the parents.

First play: *The Room* (1957)

ACROSS

1 Supplemented, with "out"
5 *Mutiny on the Bounty* coauthor
9 Snag a fly
14 Plumb __
15 Bread spread
16 *Ten North Frederick* author
17 Piccadilly statue
18 *Starlight Express* setting
19 Cameroon neighbor
20 Pinter play
23 Workout establishment
24 Chinese "way"
25 Mother of Zephyrus
26 __ de deux
28 Equipment
30 Poe animal
35 Bornean, e.g.
37 Ibsen character
38 Singer Guthrie
39 Pinter play
42 Levin et al.
43 Sushi-bar selections
44 Literary uncle
45 *The Burning Glass* poet
47 Trivial
48 Poet Hughes
49 Immense time period
50 Cry audibly
53 Hot __ pistol
56 Pinter play
60 Ferber novel
62 Actress Swenson
63 Mr. O'Casey
64 "Common Sense" writer
65 Trash hauler
66 As to
67 *Inside the Third Reich* author
68 Armored vehicle
69 Iambs and spondees

DOWN

1 Choose a candidate
2 *M*A*S*H* setting
3 Of interest to Rachel Carson
4 One a day, perhaps
5 Stephen King genre
6 Twain or Saki
7 Penitential period
8 God of mischief
9 Fine brandy
10 "Eureka!"
11 Keep __ on (watch)
12 Trim, as a photo
13 Mandlikova of tennis
21 Bingo relative
22 Type of abstract paintings
27 Brinker, e.g.
29 Annoys
30 "__ Street Blues"
31 Not as many
32 Spot for Poirot
33 Baseball family name
34 Large amount
35 Zealous
36 Horse's father
37 Docking place
40 Enjoys Emerson
41 "You __ serious?"
46 Scanty
47 Edmonds novel setting
49 Instigate
51 Chicago airport
52 "John Brown's Body" poet
53 African menaces
54 Bars near sinks
55 Rose Mary Murphy's love
57 Shopper's reference
58 __ *Gold* (Cussler novel)
59 What "quasi" means
61 Nectar ender

He began his career as an actor.

His first full-length play was *The Birthday Party*.

He wrote the screenplay for *The French Lieutenant's Woman*.

"Cynicism is an unpleasant way of saying the truth."

ACROSS

1 Two quarters of football
5 "High Hopes" lyricist
9 "The Impossible __"
14 Evangelist Roberts
15 Jai __
16 "Old MacDonald" refrain
17 They're stolen in the play
20 One of the Magi
21 "Winning __ everything"
22 Sportscaster's shout
23 "Try me!"
25 Recipe abbr.
27 Catharine of Aragon's daughter
30 *My Saber Is Bent* author
32 Bit of gossip
36 "__ Got Sixpence"
37 African fly
39 Corporate identifier
40 With 42 Across, author of the play
42 See 40 Across
44 *Inter* __ (among other things)
45 Memorable Dracula
47 Baltimore summer setting: Abbr.
48 Formula for salt
49 Phone letters
50 Extremely inconvenient
52 *A Room of One's* __
54 Certain soft drinks
56 Paul Bunyan's blacksmith
59 Waffle brand
61 Engraves deeply
65 Character in the play
68 Hapless sort
69 Plane-related
70 Part of New York's northern border
71 *Golf Begins at Forty* author
72 Sounds of reproach
73 Try out for a part

DOWN

1 __ Kong
2 Purview
3 Brings up the rear
4 Potter rabbit
5 Where *Aïda* premiered
6 Like
7 Natural environment
8 Actor Asther
9 Red ink
10 __ Grande
11 Meeny preceder
12 Assistant
13 George S. collaborator
18 *Bounty* stop
19 Main courses
24 Become talkative
26 Medicinal form
27 La Scala locale
28 St. Theresa's home
29 Artifact
31 Off the ship
33 Heavy volumes
34 Archaic exclamation
35 Ike's British colleague
38 See 66 Down
41 French composer
43 Boundaries
46 Chromosome sets
51 Optical-illusion artist
53 __ Sisters (*Macbeth* witches)
55 Foot-long sandwiches
56 Barn birds
57 Androcles associate
58 Differently
60 Exam for some coll. seniors
62 *The Absence of War* playwright
63 Lamb alias
64 Toboggan
66 With 38 Down, *Miss Saigon* Tony winner
67 Gopherwood boat

The amount of 17 Across is $88,000.

The original cast included Tallulah Bankhead.

1	2	3	4		5	6	7	8		9	10	11	12	13
14					15					16				
17				18				19						
20						21				22				
			23		24		25		26				
27	28	29			30		31		32	33	34	35
36				37	38				39				
40			41				42	43					
44				45		46				47			
48				49				50	51				
			52	53		54		55					
56	57	58		59		60		61		62	63	64
65			66				67						
68					69				70				
71					72				73				

Another Part of the Forest is a prequel to the play.

27 MACBETH (1606)

"Out, damned spot! Out, I say!"

ACROSS

1 Calliope, for one
5 Specify
9 Global extremes
14 Electrical units
15 Square footage
16 "__ Grow Up" (*Peter Pan* tune)
17 Corp. head
18 Spanish rivers
19 Make joyful
20 Witches' brew ingredient
22 Shelley concern
23 *Lorenzo's* __
24 *A Lost Lady* author
25 Charybdis colleague
29 "Tam O'Shanter" poet
31 Shun
32 Buster Brown's dog
33 Will-o'-the-__
37 City in Austria
38 Duke or earl
39 Word form for "thought"
40 Verdi masterwork
41 Paris airport
42 Government security, for short
43 Cologne's river
45 Milne character
46 Macbeth's thanedom
49 Canine sound
50 Keats, e.g.
51 Witches' brew ingredient
57 Confuse
58 "__ Ben Adhem"
59 Detroit product
60 *Answered Prayers* author
61 Fish features
62 Declined
63 Ice handlers
64 Trial
65 Hardy title character

DOWN

1 Sulk
2 *Driving Miss Daisy* author
3 Barrie character
4 Exxon's ex-name
5 C.S. Lewis land
6 Prospero's servant
7 Feline comment
8 Cardinal point
9 Merchant of rhyme
10 Witches' brew ingredient
11 Not at all eager
12 French preposition
13 Cowboys' concern
21 Throw in one's hand
24 Canadian Indian
25 *Casa* room
26 107, in old Rome
27 "__ Cassius has a lean and hungry look"
28 Witches' brew ingredient
29 All-time bestselling book
30 *The __ American*
32 Unable to decide
34 Pedestal figure
35 Locale
36 __ laureate
38 Black: Fr.
42 Minor quarrel
44 Monopoly pieces
45 *Swann's Way* author
46 Move via momentum
47 Augment
48 Augment
49 Extremely long time
51 Wilson's predecessor
52 *Village Voice* award
53 *Freedom Road* author
54 Precept
55 Elevator inventor
56 Valhalla VIPs

THE MAN WHO CAME TO DINNER (1939)

"Go in and read the life of Florence Nightingale and learn how unfitted you are for your chosen profession."

ACROSS

1 Luxurious
5 Remove, as a hat
9 Literary rep
14 In __ of (instead of)
15 Weena, for one
16 Poet Jones
17 With 57 Across, inspiration for the title character
19 Soda flavor
20 Du Maurier novel
21 Fly weapon
23 Pitchfork parts
24 President, at times
26 Quichelike
27 '60s racehorse
28 Until
32 Encouraging touches
33 ... And __ of the Club
35 Feeling green
39 *City of the Beasts* author
40 Bisected
41 Fr. women
42 Hubris, e.g.
43 Hatfield enemy
45 Sport fish
49 Spheres of influence
51 *Funny Girl* subject
52 Dante masterwork
55 Fairy king
56 Goddess of the hunt
57 See 17 Across
60 *Beowulf* and *The Iliad*
61 *The Right Stuff* focus
62 Bantu people
63 Lauder of cosmetics
64 Dumbfound
65 Feature of some autos

DOWN

1 Omaha's river
2 Drilling device
3 Recognizing
4 *Antic Hay* author
5 Declare untrue
6 Medieval
7 Antagonist
8 Winning positions
9 Swimming-pool problem
10 With 38 Down, inspiration for Lorraine Sheldon in the play
11 Part of QED
12 "Uh-uh!"
13 Management level
18 Belly muscles
22 Original portrayer of the title character
24 Memorial Day marchers
25 Overhead trains
27 Coauthor of the play, with Hart
29 Brooch
30 Senator Kennedy
31 Suffix for sugars
32 Officeholder
34 Jolson et al.
35 Skippy competitor
36 Blow up a photo: Abbr.
37 "Gotcha!"
38 See 10 Down
39 Old Testament prophet
41 End of the 19th century
44 *A Thousand __*
45 *The Threepenny Opera* author
46 Ventilate
47 Opera star Renata
48 Parodied
50 Strike out
51 Tanker unit: Abbr.
52 __ *fixe*
53 Small bites
54 __ accompli
55 *The Good Earth* character
58 Bran source
59 Columbus sch.

The play is dedicated to 17 Across, "for reasons that are nobody's business."

The character Banjo is based on Harpo Marx.

The play is set in Mesalia, Ohio.

29 A MIDSUMMER NIGHT'S DREAM (1596)

"The course of true love never did run smooth."

ACROSS

1 *The Day of the Locust* author
5 Mars alias
9 *Twenty Years* __
14 Mental image
15 Hernando's home
16 Australian native
17 Atty.-to-be's exam
18 Ledger examiners: Abbr.
19 Archie Bunker persona
20 Pursuer of Hermia in the play
22 Obliterate
23 Golf star Ernie
24 Color
25 Take a crack at
26 When Churchill was a POW
29 Office fill-in
33 Elate
36 Make tracks
37 Lotion additive
38 Puck's other name
42 *If __ the Zoo* (Seuss book)
43 Plural pronoun
44 Peruses
45 Explosive sound
46 Lesage novel
49 Tango need
51 Away from the office
52 *The Tale of a* __ (Swift work)
55 Ezra Pound's birthplace
58 Amazon queen in the play
61 Hermia, to Lysander
62 Popular cookie
63 Landed
64 Curved line
65 Soothsayer's observance
66 Soccer great
67 Contributed
68 Paper repairer
69 Stowe book

DOWN

1 Dorian Gray creator
2 Henry Ford's son
3 Pants borders
4 British poet Nahum
5 What interest may do
6 Sporting sword
7 Jacob's brother
8 Fresh talk
9 Traffic-light color
10 Grimm fare
11 *Julius Caesar* costume
12 Winged god
13 Baptism, for one
21 *The __ Birds*
25 Not kosher
26 Kosinski novel
27 Fingerprint pattern
28 __ and abet
30 Logan of *Finian's Rainbow*
31 Frame of mind
32 Abbey seating
33 Baby's bed
34 Circle dance
35 *Diplomacy for the Next Century* author
39 Enthusiastic
40 George Sand's assent
41 Sister of Euterpe
47 Shepherdess of rhyme
48 First Broadway Evita
50 Pulitzer's New York paper
52 *The Accidental Tourist* author
53 Serving a purpose
54 With __ breath
55 *Casablanca* character
56 *Harvey* hero
57 Zealous
58 Least bit of concern
59 *My Friend* __
60 *Dragnet* org.

The "play within a play" is
Pyramus and Thisbe.

Bottom
the
weaver is
its lead
player.

Other fairies include Peaseblossom,
Cobweb and Mustardseed.

30 WILLIAM SHAKESPEARE

First play: *Henry VI* (c. 1591)

ACROSS

1 Three-note chord
6 Author Hoffer
10 Tom Sawyer transportation
14 Actress Zellweger
15 Lie around
16 Kon-Tiki Museum locale
17 Imitative sorts
18 Scott of *Happy Days*
19 Head the cast
20 Shakespeare play
22 *The __ of Four* (Sherlock Holmes novel)
23 Probate concern
24 Trivial
26 Weaving machines
29 Make out
33 Shelley selection
36 Incursion
38 Author Calvino
39 Shakespeare play
43 Infuriated
44 Type of tide
45 "__ under the haystack . . ."
46 *Arabian Nights* magic word
48 Emulate Fagin
51 Trumpeter Al
53 Barbecues
57 Where Kashmir is
60 Shakespeare play
63 Halo, for example
64 Listen to
65 Knightly activities
66 *Eleni* author
67 Watermelon covering
68 Objects of adoration
69 Augury
70 Overfill
71 Batsman of rhyme

DOWN

1 Go a gumshoe's job
2 Taken-back autos
3 Nonreactive
4 Skybound
5 Mississippi explorer
6 Island near Capri
7 Speckled horse
8 "Topless towers" place
9 Shuttered
10 Poet family surname
11 __ spumante
12 Jolly Roger, for one
13 Lacerated
21 Mrs. Arrowsmith
25 Rider's strap
27 *Joseph and His Brothers* author
28 Flanks
30 Priced individually
31 Colonel Mustard's game
32 Play with horseshoes
33 "Miss __ Regrets"
34 Harrowing
35 Greek letters
37 "Darn it!"
40 *The Country Girl* Tony winner
41 Tractor-trailer
42 *Macbeth* or *Otello*
47 Mishaps in a Shakespearean comedy
49 Of a major artery
50 *Annie Hall* catchphrase
52 Leg bone
54 Grain buildings
55 Words on a spine
56 Wimp
57 Mythical ship
58 Rodgers and Hammerstein setting
59 *Splendor in the Grass* author
61 *The Seven-Per-__ Solution*
62 Stevenson character

Shakespeare is credited with the
authorship of 37 plays.

He has
1,960
listings in
the 16th
edition of
Bartlett's
Familiar
Quotations.

The King James Bible is in second place,
with 1,591.

31 THE MIRACLE WORKER (1959)

"She is like a little safe, locked, that no one can open."

ACROSS

1 Part of Addams' signature
5 Canine comments
9 *A __ Grows in Brooklyn*
13 Quiet partner
14 Porgy's transportation
15 "The __ of Tralee"
16 Poisonous snake
17 Russian ruler of old
18 W.H. Hudson character
19 Original cast member of the play
22 Detective, often
23 Bar entertainment
27 Genesis character
30 Subject of the play
31 Iwo Jima fighting force: Abbr.
34 "Huh?"
36 Like an ingénue
37 Belgian resort
38 Setting of the play
40 Old __ (London theatre)
41 Activated, as an explosive
43 Actress Garr
44 Bit of progress
45 Author of the play
47 *Chicago* character
49 Self-indulgent exercise
51 Blackbirds' place
55 Original cast member of the play
58 TV tower
61 Disraeli title
62 Hair coloring
63 Suffix for kitchen
64 Nursery school, for short
65 These, in Cádiz
66 Stocking stuffers
67 __ *Breckinridge*
68 Proofer's marking

DOWN

1 Furniture wood
2 Was compelled
3 Like Mencken's wit
4 *Hardy Boys* or *Nancy Drew*
5 Play starter
6 Tabula __
7 Teen diarist
8 Flash of lightning
9 Singing syllables
10 Thieve
11 Compass reading
12 Sargasso Sea swimmer
13 New York Shakespeare Festival founder
20 Swimming stroke
21 *In the __* (Nixon book)
24 Salad ingredient
25 Actor Spacey
26 Do construction work
28 *The Man Who Mistook His Wife for __*
29 Highland Games need
31 Lexicographer's concern
32 Piece of parsley
33 Cha-cha alternative
35 Poi source
38 Festoon
39 Add and stir
42 Societal strata
44 *Mommie __*
46 Prime-time hour
48 Tape-measure markings
50 *Nearest the Pole* author
52 Bridge, in Bologna
53 Alternatively
54 Athenian vowels
56 Rabbit or Fox's title
57 __-Seltzer
58 Bumped into
59 From __ Z
60 Eye annoyance

The play is the Official Outdoor Drama
of 38 Across.

45 Across
based his
play on
30 Across'
auto-
biography.

A TV version of the play was shown on
Playhouse 90 two years before its
Broadway debut.

32 THE MISANTHROPE (1666)

"She shows her zeal in every holy place, but still she's vain enough to paint her face."

ACROSS

1 Author of the play
8 Character in the play
15 Mistaken
16 Hangs around
17 Cyrano's love
18 Veteran sailor
19 Aunt: Sp.
20 *Bury My Heart at Wounded __*
21 Shoe part
22 Check casher
25 Requirements
26 Roll with the punches
27 Chicken __ king
28 Actress Kerr
31 Character in the play
34 Has being
38 Leon Uris novel
39 *The Cocktail Party* author
40 *Tatler* collaborator
41 Character in the play
42 Like Omar
44 Road-service org.
45 "__ we forget . . ."
48 Courtroom VIP
49 Something extra
51 Bank-acct. posting
52 Haywire
54 Sheep sound
55 Took along
57 *Their Eyes Were Watching God* author
61 *Ralph __ Doister* (earliest known English comedy)
62 *Goosebumps* author
63 Character in the play
64 Character in the play

DOWN

1 Peace, to Tolstoy
2 Yoko __
3 Superman foe Luthor
4 In a huff
5 WWII correspondent Pyle
6 Author Jaffe
7 Poet's preposition
8 *The Tempest* 9 Down
9 Play part
10 Show partiality
11 Part of TGIF
12 "Terrif!"
13 Ship deck
14 Mary Kay competitor
20 Japanese port
22 Treaties
23 Wide awake
24 Cole Porter, circa 1910
25 Forswear
26 Spicy dish
28 Discourage
29 Lucite, for instance
30 Skater's leap
32 Not skillful
33 Runner's distance
35 Biblical peak
36 Bottom line
37 Great bargain
39 *The Powers __ Be* (Halberstam book)
41 Sympathetic feeling
43 *Being and Nothingness* author
45 Only inanimate zodiac sign
46 Register
47 Zeno follower
49 Language of Iran
50 Dreadlocks wearer
52 Catalysts: Abbr.
53 Sharpen
54 Papal decree
56 Find a job for
57 Otho's domain: Abbr.
58 Kitchen-wrap metal
59 N.Y. neighbor
60 Wedding-announcement word

The title character is 63 Across.

He is in
love with
31 Across.

41 Across is a friend of 63 Across.

"What's this crud about there being no movie tonight?"

ACROSS

1 Reduce drastically
6 Compact __
10 *The Art of the Fugue* composer
14 Excessive speed
15 Ancient South American
16 Shampoo ingredient
17 Ore test
18 "Cabbages" or "kings"
19 Poet Sandburg
20 Original cast member of the play
22 Peeling potatoes, perhaps
23 Dove sound
24 Hotbed
26 Coauthor of the play
32 Golf instructor
35 The Charles' dog
36 Ancient Chinese poet
37 Dish's fellow traveler
39 Henry VIII's VIth
40 Isadora Duncan's undoing
42 Pioneer automaker
43 Japanese canine
45 *Picnic* character
46 64 Across, for one
47 Siesta
48 Item thrown overboard in the play
51 Actor Beatty
52 *Please Don't __ the Daisies*
53 From Bangkok
56 Original cast member of the play
63 *Harpo Speaks!* author
64 Film role for 20 Across
65 Laker or Celtic
66 Conclusion preceder
67 "__ bigger and better things!"
68 *Oklahoma!* aunt
69 Inert gas
70 *I Loves You, Porgy* singer
71 Real-estate documents

DOWN

1 Persian ruler
2 Omit coherent light
3 Special-interest grp.
4 Astronomical diagram
5 Attention getter
6 Rat Pack member
7 Get __ the ground floor
8 Gulf War missile
9 Mazo de la Roche's homeland
10 *Novum Organum* author
11 Astronaut Shepard
12 Irish port
13 Lend a hand
21 Mares' offspring
25 Pulver's rank: Abbr.
26 *Rising Sun* setting
27 City in 26 Down
28 Landing area
29 Permissible
30 Eye-bending paintings
31 Steve Lawrence's wife
32 European dance
33 *Le Penseur* creator
34 Beginning
38 Bar amenity
41 No longer bright
44 Boulle beast
49 James Bond adversary
50 Got a loan for, perhaps
51 *No More Vietnams* author
53 Secret Service agents, e.g.
54 Rabbit relative
55 Golden Fleece transporter
57 Topnotch
58 Fermenting tanks
59 Wedding exchanges
60 Sinclair Lewis alma mater
61 Requisite
62 Slips up

The title character's first name is Doug.

The play is set on the cargo ship *Reluctant*.

The other coauthor was Thomas Heggen, who wrote the novel upon which the play was based.

34 THE ODD COUPLE (1965)

"In other words, you're throwing me out." "Not in other words. Those are the perfect ones."

ACROSS

1 Numerical prefix
5 *My Wide World* autobiographer
10 On __ with (equivalent to)
14 Escutcheon stain
15 Present an address
16 Verse, alternatively
17 Actress Hatcher
18 Makes a scene
19 Ottoman governors
20 Original cast member of the play
22 Left-ventricle outlet
23 Sundial numeral
24 Mincemeat creation
25 Poker-player role in the play
26 Sabres and Bruins
28 Noble act
30 Printer's widths
31 Do well at retail
32 *Café* order
34 Original cast member of the play
39 *Green Eggs and Ham* kid
40 B&Bs
42 End of Horner's boast
45 Yuletide
46 Adhesive note name
48 Poker-player role in the play
50 Hyannis entrée
51 ". . . __ woodchuck could chuck wood"
52 Drawings: Abbr.
53 Author of the play
56 Slightly
57 Rita Hayworth role
58 Twine
59 Vocal inflection
60 William White's middle name
61 "This one's __!"
62 Means justifiers
63 Cookbook author James
64 Big Board initials

DOWN

1 Acquires
2 Humorous poem
3 __ *Flat* (Steinbeck novel)
4 Of hearing
5 Author West
6 *The Red Badge of Courage* author
7 __ *and Abel*
8 Counselor: Abbr.
9 Unquestionably
10 Ann __, MI
11 Author Boulle
12 *The Joy Luck Club* author
13 States differently
21 Spr. month
22 Sit in on a class
25 Potatoes partner
27 House extensions
28 *Camille* author
29 Ancient Mideast kingdom
32 "Summertime," for one
33 "Memories Are Made of __"
35 Airport lineup
36 Plus-size supermodel
37 Metallic element
38 *Mister Roberts* costumes
41 Train commuter, at times
42 Emulate Earhart
43 *Paradise Lost* writer
44 Not coastal
46 Jerzy Kosinski's birthplace
47 "__ bodkins!"
49 Some Rubens works
50 *The __ House Rules*
53 Cleopatra's river
54 Actress Raines
55 Religious symbol
57 Shoot the breeze

Felix's last name is Ungar in the play,
and Unger in the TV series.

The
original
Broadway
production
was
directed by
Mike
Nichols.

A female version, starring Rita Moreno
and Sally Struthers, made its Broadway
debut in 1985.

35 SAM SHEPARD

First plays: *Cowboys* and *The Rock Garden* (1964)

ACROSS

1 Simon Legree creator
6 *Cabaret* name
10 Loath to work
14 Melodic
15 Quote-book abbr.
16 *Peter and the Wolf* duck
17 Shepard play
20 Whispered sound
21 Vitamin amts.
22 Exemplar of greed
23 Blunted blade
25 Golfer's pocketful
27 Shepard play
31 *Bleak House* character
34 Sir __ Newton
35 Site of the William Tell legend
36 Yemeni city
37 Acoustician's nightmare
38 Oscar winner as Sophie
40 *The __ Piper of Hamelin*
41 Supplemented, with "out"
42 Chemical suffix
43 Mimicry
44 Teen's exclamation
45 Shepard play
48 Capital of West Germany
49 Wine's bouquet
50 Dannay/Lee pseudonym
53 Scandinavian city
55 Ambush
59 Shepard play
62 Captive of Hercules
63 *Star Wars* princess
64 Sister of Cordelia
65 __ Ed.
66 Network owned by Disney
67 "Leda and the Swan" author

DOWN

1 Footfall
2 Hula hoops and Frisbees
3 Small bills
4 With *The*, T.S. Eliot poem
5 Santa Claus, to Moore
6 Pantry
7 Pizarro victim
8 With *The*, Albee play
9 *Finnegans Wake* character
10 Author Auchincloss
11 Not yet arisen
12 *Nana* author
13 Roll-call tally
18 Droxie alternative
19 Captain Hook aide
24 One-striper: Abbr.
26 Malevolent
27 Dietary component
28 Honshu metropolis
29 Propelled a scull
30 Drew in
31 Fancy farewell
32 Plow man
33 Rooney et al.
36 With *The*, Alan Alda musical of '66
38 Intend
39 Chapter extras
43 Stomach muscles
45 Stereo ancestor
46 Borrowed, as a museum piece
47 Erratum
48 __ *noires*
50 Stick it in your ear!
51 "Yipes!"
52 Counting syllable
54 *Bounty* or *Pequod*
56 Capital of Latvia
57 *Amo, amas*, __
58 Writes
60 Flamenco cheer
61 __, *the Beloved Country*

His real last name is Rogers.

He portrayed Chuck Yeager in the film *The Right Stuff*.

He won a Pulitzer Prize for his 1979 play *Buried Child*.

"Blessed be the tie that binds."

ACROSS

1 Social misfit
5 Strong wind
9 Rice style
14 Phone company employee: Abbr.
15 Norwegian royal name
16 43 Down service
17 Informal greeting
18 Mrs. Nick Charles
19 *Midnight Cowboy* character
20 Married couple in the play
23 Toothbrush brand
24 Impresario Hurok
25 Author Buntline
26 Actor Le__ Burton
27 *Picnic* author
31 Pensive comment
33 Cathedral area
35 Scourge
37 Not together
41 Narrator of the play
44 "Self-Reliance" is one
45 Arsenal contents
46 Fuji competitor
47 Increases
49 Ivy League school
51 Agent, for short
52 Balaam's beast
55 John, in Scotland
57 Hideouts
59 Author of the play
64 Make obscure
65 Maugham work
66 Bird, in 11 Down
68 Vowel sequence
69 Tie fabric
70 Cultured fellow
71 Chaplin persona
72 Jed Clampett's daughter
73 Feeling tense

DOWN

1 Japanese drama
2 Chapter-starting quotations
3 Prepares for a premiere
4 Betray anticipation
5 *Amateur Hour* prop
6 Succulent plant
7 Zhivago's love
8 *The American Century* author
9 *Westward Ha!* author
10 Muslim cleric
11 Livy's language
12 Usher's path
13 Aviator Bennett
21 Baseball stat
22 Homer Simpson exclamation
23 Roundish
28 Hoop group: Abbr.
29 Smitten
30 *An __ of the People* (Ibsen play)
32 Movie-rating org.
34 Biblical birthright seller
36 Poet Lazarus
38 Wronged
39 Making a citation
40 Golf hazards
42 Readying a manuscript
43 EarthLink alternative
48 Emulated Miss Muffet
50 Plumber's joint
52 Baseball stat
53 Out-and-out
54 European capital
56 Branch of mythology
58 "A fool and his money . . .", e.g.
60 Conservatory or library
61 Polish target
62 Shakespeare nickname
63 Deep black
67 Farm enclosure

The play is set in Grover's Corners,
New Hampshire.

41 Across
speaks
directly to
the
audience.

The play covers the period 1901-1913.

37 PLAY IT AGAIN, SAM (1969)

"Dames are simple. I never met one that didn't understand a slap in the mouth or a slug from a .45."

ACROSS

1 Depart from the script
6 Ichabod's rival
10 Editor's notation
14 Fictional Swiss miss
15 Singer McEntire
16 401(k) alternatives
17 Main character of the play
19 Pretentiousness
20 Wet, as some lawns
21 As the script indicates
22 *Ghost Beach* author
26 *Out of Africa* author
28 Irish statesman De Valera
29 Adidas alternative
31 Takes along
33 Slugger's number
34 Caesarean phrase
38 Like some crowds
39 *Heart of Darkness* character
41 At the drop of __
42 Soothsayer
43 WWII area
44 Give testimony
46 Bay windows
49 Wake up
50 *The Carpetbaggers* author
53 *The Last Hurrah* author
55 Actress Burstyn
56 Task-force job: Abbr.
57 Way in
58 Author of the play
64 "__ Rhythm"
65 Hawaiian figurine
66 Silents star Pola
67 Exercise centers
68 Vehicle on runners
69 Author Madame de __

DOWN

1 Cry of discovery
2 Andrea __ Sarto
3 Like Abner
4 Muckraker Tarbell
5 Book part
6 "Phrase and Fable" dictionary compiler
7 Bank (on)
8 Sapporo sash
9 Grinch's dog
10 Original cast member of the play
11 Ambler et al.
12 Oater star Lash
13 Ruhr Valley city
18 Swampland
21 "Sail __ Ship of State!"
22 Picture puzzle
23 T-shirt size
24 Show enjoyment
25 Original cast member of the play
26 Something to pay
27 Majorca neighbor
30 Robin portrayer in '38
32 Bundle of yarn
35 Annan's organization
36 *Jerusalem Delivered* poet
37 Speak
40 Salt Lake City collegians
45 *Iliad* warriors
47 __ Tin Tin
48 Unseemly
50 Do more research
51 Scientific study
52 Fictional Leopold
54 Less than straightforward
56 Pig's proverbial place
58 Lbs. and ozs.
59 Peanut product
60 *Live and __ Die*
61 Airport near JFK
62 Homophone for air
63 Zilch

10 Down and 25 Down repeated their roles in the film version.

1	2	3	4	5		6	7	8	9		10	11	12	13
14						15					16			
17					18						19			
				20						21				
22	23	24	25				26	27						
28						29	30							
31				32		33				34	35	36	37	
38				39	40					41				
42				43				44	45					
			46	47			48		49					
50	51	52					53	54						
55						56								
57					58	59				60	61	62	63	
64				65				66						
67				68				69						

58 Across once counted that the play got 155 laughs.

In its first London run, 17 Across was portrayed by Dudley Moore.

38 PYGMALION (1913)

"The difference between a lady and a flower girl is not how she behaves, but how she's treated."

ACROSS

1 *Fried Green Tomatoes...* author
6 Unappetizing meal
10 Boxer's weapon
14 Perry's assistant
15 Abominable Snowman
16 Charley horse
17 Become ready to pick
18 Top of the head
19 Blue shade
20 Freddy's last name in the play
23 Run in
26 *Seven Days in __*
27 Stage settings
28 Tarzan's peers
30 Creative talent
32 Typist's asset
33 Kind of test
34 Boathouse item
37 Eliza's father in the play
41 French article
42 Two less than *drei*
43 *Expensive People* author
44 Hard to see
46 Royal __ Hall (London landmark)
47 Pu-yi's capital
50 Pie __ mode
51 ACLU concern
52 Pickering's pal in the play
56 Trojan War instigator
57 Conflicted
58 Rose protector
62 River deposit
63 Nebraska Indian
64 *Ah Sin* author
65 Electrified fish
66 Xanthippe et al.
67 Fix deeply

DOWN

1 *Sunrise at Campobello* subject
2 Floral necklace
3 Eiger, for one
4 High spirits
5 Cupbearer of the gods
6 Styne/Sondheim musical
7 Creator of Ferdinand the Bull
8 *My Ántonia* character
9 *Fear Strikes Out* author
10 Laertes, to Odysseus
11 Strand, perhaps
12 Oil source
13 Blabs
21 Bert Bobbsey's sister
22 Start of the 7th century
23 __ congestion
24 Pie filling
25 Makes a complaint
29 *L'Invasion de la __* (Verne novel)
30 Call to a bellhop
31 Vietnam neighbor
33 Chief Norse god
34 Ermine relative
35 On the ball
36 Takes a break
38 *Funeral in Berlin* author
39 Gilbert and Sullivan operetta
40 File projection
44 They happened earliest
45 Whichever
46 __ Baba
47 Half moon, e.g.
48 Macabre
49 Sad sound
50 Mame's secretary
53 Tiny amount
54 Pirate's quaff
55 False front
59 Eye, poetically
60 Numbered rd.
61 *The Age of Innocence* character

Leslie Howard portrayed 52 Across in
the 1938 film version.

George
Bernard
Shaw's
screenplay
won an
Academy
Award.

52 Across first sees Eliza outside the
Royal Opera House in Covent Garden.

39 A RAISIN IN THE SUN (1959)

"There is always something left to love. And if you ain't learned that, you ain't learned nothing."

ACROSS

1 Term of endearment
5 Hymn finale
9 Parcel out
14 Fencing sword
15 Eco's farewell
16 Blackmore heroine
17 See 11 Down
19 Be of one mind
20 Set of principles
21 Bandleader Brown
23 Time periods
24 Moo __ pork
25 *Silent Spring* subject
28 Additive total
30 Munich exclamation
31 Beginner
33 Train lines: Abbr.
35 Mexican leader Juárez
37 First male action figure
39 World Wide Web
40 Original cast member of the play
43 Run of wins
44 Baggage attachment
45 Out-of-the-way place
46 Be indisposed
47 Hamilton sleuth
51 Shakespearean prince
52 Em preceder
54 Elec. charge
56 Grassland
57 *Broadway My Way* recording artist
59 *The Producers* character
61 Gasket
63 1507, on cornerstones
65 Original cast member of the play
68 *Silas Marner* author
69 Actress Lollobrigida
70 *The __ Next Time* (Baldwin book)
71 Start of an Austen title
72 Super-sharp video offering: Abbr.
73 Worry

DOWN

1 Command
2 Lack of interest
3 Lew Wallace novel
4 __ *Can* (Sammy Davis, Jr. book)
5 Expert
6 Peace, to Tolstoy
7 James __ Jones
8 "The Highwayman" poet
9 Orthodontists' org.
10 Theater level
11 With 17 Across, author of the play
12 Play without an intermission
13 Golfer's starter
18 A followers
22 *A Tale of the Christ*, for 3 Down
26 Fictional scientist
27 Priam's kingdom
29 Conductor Zubin
32 Poet Nash
34 Photo tone
36 Horse sound
38 Preposterous
40 Be undecided
41 *The Boys From Brazil* author
42 Owner of Sleipnir
43 Connives
48 Cure-all
49 Poe woman
50 Refrigerator attachment
53 Olivier ex
55 Fourth word of the Old Testament
58 Ocho __, Jamaica
60 *Metamorphoses* writer
62 Jazz phrase
64 Mineral suffix
66 Aesop animal
67 Of sea forces: Abbr.

This was the first play written, directed
and performed by African-Americans to
run for over 500 performances on
Broadway.

The title
comes
from a
Langston
Hughes
poem.

Other original cast members included
Ruby Dee and Louis Gossett.

1	2	3	4		5	6	7	8		9	10	11	12	13
14					15					16				
17				18						19				
20						21		22		23				
24			25	26	27		28		29		30			
31			32		33		34		35		36			
			37	38						39				
	40	41					42							
43						44								
45						46			47	48	49	50		
51				52		53		54		55		56		
57			58		59		60			61	62			
63			64		65		66	67						
68					69				70					
71					72				73					

First play: *Come Blow Your Horn* (1961)

ACROSS

1 Like some tongues
5 Small dogs
10 One way to leave the ground
14 Built
15 San Antonio landmark
16 Film rating org.
17 Simon play
20 *Escargot*
21 "Minuet __"
22 Charged
23 *The Longest Day* author
25 Back area
27 Simon play
31 Use a sickle
35 Japanese belt
36 Antitoxins
37 Sapid
39 Brief time
41 Ref. set
43 Fishing gear
44 Not at all enthusiastic
46 Thumbs-down votes
48 Codswallop
49 *From __ to Eternity*
50 Simon play
53 "Scram!"
55 Together, in music
56 *Sunset Boulevard* star on Broadway
59 Sindbad transport
61 Bacon unit
65 Simon play
68 Squared off
69 Spender and Spenser
70 Thruways, e.g.: Abbr.
71 Actress Swenson
72 Serving pieces
73 *The Mysterious Island* captain

DOWN

1 Qtys.
2 *High Button Shoes* lyricist
3 Notion
4 __ *Under the Elms*
5 Cooking utensil
6 Hamlet's home
7 *The Boys of Summer* author
8 Expatriate
9 Biff, to Willy
10 *The Admirable Crichton* author
11 "Once __ a midnight dreary"
12 Writer Angelou
13 Sandburg's "bucket of ashes"
18 Controversial Joyce book
19 Baseball statistic
24 Reverential feeling
26 Pilot's heading: Abbr.
27 Old Testament book
28 Overhead
29 Baseball great Ralph
30 Divine nourishment
32 Film critic Roger
33 Permit
34 Green sauce
38 *On Beyond Zebra* author
40 Shakespearean title character
42 What a theater can hold
45 *The Name of the Rose* author
47 Since Jan. 1
51 *Frankenstein* genre
52 *The __ of the Native*
54 Magazine publisher's nickname
56 One-fifth of MXXX
57 Reclined
58 Designer Cassini
60 Highest draft rating
62 Religious ceremony
63 Menu listing
64 Mexican coin
66 __ for (choose)
67 Stubborn beast

His full name is Marvin Neil Simon.

1	2	3	4	█	5	6	7	8	9	█	10	11	12	13
14				█	15					█	16			
17				18						19				
20				█	21			█	22					
█	█	█	23		24		█	25	26			█	█	█
27	28	29				30			█	31	32	33	34
35			█	36			█	37	38				
39			40		█	41		42	█	43			
44				45	█	46		47	█	48			
49			█	50	51				█	52			
█	█	█	53	54			█	55				█	█	█
56	57	58			█	59	60	█	61		62	63	64
65				█	66			67					
68			█	69			█	70				
71			█	72			█	73				

He received Kennedy Center Honors in 1995.

His *Brighton Beach Memoirs* character Eugene Jerome is based on himself.

41 ROMEO AND JULIET (c. 1595)

"O! I am Fortune's fool."

ACROSS

1 Ancient Greek epic
6 Poetic foot
10 Rhyme scheme
14 Conductor's concerns
15 Canadian Indian
16 Czech city
17 "A pair of __ lovers" (Prologue)
19 Mare meal
20 Old-time pronoun
21 Author Kesey
22 Cole Porter's last musical score
24 Nourished
25 *The Unanswered Question* composer
26 "She speaks, yet she __" (Act II, Scene II)
32 Appliance-store display
35 Reviews galleys
36 Learning method
37 Not care __
38 Prefix for second
39 Brutus or Cassius
40 Soccer great
41 Button alternative
42 Daredevil Knievel
43 Vowel mark
44 Geologic time unit
45 "Gallop apace, you __ steeds" (Act III, Scene II)
47 Become boring
49 __ Saud
50 Hot stuff
53 Initials for Queen Elizabeth
54 *Evita* narrator
57 Spoken
58 "That I shall say good night till __" (Act II, Scene II)
61 Long (for)
62 Agcy. created by Eisenhower
63 *The Power of Positive Thinking* author
64 The __ of Concord (Emerson)
65 Gratified
66 Oscar relatives

DOWN

1 __-bitsy
2 Mother of Apollo
3 One-named supermodel
4 Equinox mo.
5 *Our Mutual Friend* author
6 Cathedral relic
7 __ *Poetica*
8 *Black __* (Zane Grey novel)
9 Sheets and pillowcases
10 Home
11 Massachusetts Bay Colony poet
12 Opponent
13 Petty officer
18 Make over
23 Norm: Abbr.
24 Camera setting
26 Logic
27 Hersey setting
28 *I Ching* pair
29 Treasure cache
30 Creator of 1 Across
31 Where 27 Down is
33 Trumpet part
34 Velocity
37 Carpenter's wear
39 On the throne
43 *I Owe Russia $1200* author
45 *Lady Windermere's __*
46 Unyielding
48 Douglas Freeman biography
50 Law enforcers
51 "Elsa's Dream," for one
52 Bibliography abbr.
53 Be in charge of
54 Pack tightly
55 Sacred
56 Wool sources
59 Merit-badge org.
60 Sleep-stage acronym

Shakespeare's source for the plot was a
narrative poem by Arthur Brooke.

1	2	3	4	5		6	7	8	9		10	11	12	13
14						15					16			
17					18						19			
20					21				22		23			
			24						25					
26	27	28				29	30	31				32	33	34
35					36					37			
38					39					40			
41					42				43				
44				45				46				
		47	48					49					
50	51				52		53				54	55	56
57				58		59			60			
61				62				63			
64				65				66			

The play
is set in
the
month of
July.

Juliet is 13 years old.

42 R.U.R. (1921)

"Everyone should buy his own robot."

ACROSS

1 Family members
6 Con games
11 Boxer's punch
14 Port of Jordan
15 "Cry '__'! and let slip . . ."
16 Completely
17 *The Burden of Proof* author
18 Green shade
19 Horner's dessert
20 General manager of R.U.R.
22 Atty.'s org.
23 Collarless shirt
24 Felix Ungar is one
26 Auditor's designation: Abbr.
29 Map lines: Abbr.
32 Sign of a sellout
33 Prom rental
35 *Harper's Bazaar* cover designer
37 Kennedy Library architect
41 R.U.R. products
44 Emerson composition
45 "__ Swell" (Rodgers and Hart tune)
46 Trade
47 Sri Lanka export
49 Arm or leg

51 Sow's spot
52 *Northwest Passage* author
56 Infant's neckwear
58 Triumphant cry
59 She marries 20 Across
65 Where Broadway is: Abbr.
66 Runyonesque pronoun
67 *Coming of Age in* __
68 Talk amorously
69 Requirements
70 Spend
71 Attila follower
72 Mores
73 Landlord's collection

DOWN

1 Walkway
2 Blue shade
3 Last wife of Henry VIII
4 Scrub a mission
5 Twain kid
6 "Scram!"
7 Self-possessed
8 Birdlike
9 What hit plays often become
10 Plot outline
11 Kōbō Abe's homeland
12 Whodunit plot element

13 __ *House* (Dickens novel)
21 Discourage
25 Pyramids, essentially
26 Colonel Mustard's game
27 Cushion's contents
28 *Lucky Jim* author
30 Prefix for while
31 Telejournalist Lesley
34 Egg-shaped
36 Blond race of fiction
38 Rambo rescuees
39 French state
40 '60s Cosby series
42 "Done," to "cone"
43 Cugat specialty
48 Went to a diner
50 Steinbeck stomping grounds
52 Reata, in *Giant*
53 "__ Beautiful Doll"
54 Baron of Verulam
55 Publisher's unsolicited manuscripts
57 Jaded
60 This: Sp.
61 Capone adversary
62 Augur's discovery
63 Defeat handily
64 Talks a lot

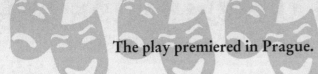

The play premiered in Prague.

Rossum, a mad scientist, discovers how to create living organisms.

The leader of the 41 Across is Radius.

43 SIX DEGREES OF SEPARATION (1990)

"He did more for us in a few hours . . . than our children ever did."

ACROSS

1 Evergreens
5 Smooth-talking
9 Windows predecessor
14 Potting soil
15 First-rate
16 In any way
17 *The Razor's __*
18 Be compelled to
19 Brazilian writer Amado
20 Star of the film version
22 Group of eight
23 Flowering shrubs
24 __ of the Covenant
25 Perfect, for one
26 Raggedy doll
28 Regarding
32 Ahab's craft
35 Peruse
36 __ Antony
40 Kind of eclipse
41 Ngaio Marsh title
42 "Goodbye, Columbus" author
43 *The Camera Never Blinks* author
45 Ingrid Bergman role
46 GI uniform
47 Tummy trouble
52 Negative vote
54 Cicero, in *Julius Caesar*
56 Overwhelms
59 Author of the play
61 Watering hole
62 Enthusiastic
63 *The __ of the Cave Bear*
64 Hippodrome
65 Trifling
66 Ritz Cracker competitor
67 DuBose Heyward novel
68 Born and __
69 Bridge seat

DOWN

1 Charged
2 Treat salt, in a way
3 Sleeve style
4 Offends the nose
5 *The Effect of __ Rays . . .*
6 Poet Untermeyer
7 Part of MIT
8 *Little Women* character
9 Barbara, for one
10 With 39 Down, star of the play
11 Move quickly
12 *The Castle* character
13 Luge
21 Percolate
24 Conductor Previn
26 Polly and Em
27 Lexicographer Webster
29 *The __ Around Us* (Carson book)
30 Robert Burns character
31 Byron selection
33 *The Jetsons* kid
34 Campus greenery
36 Med. diagnostic tool
37 "You've got mail" co.
38 ACLU concern
39 See 10 Down
44 Pealed
48 *Rive __*
49 *Napoli's* nation
50 Synagogue scrolls
51 Schoolyard retort
53 Analysis
54 Frodo's home
55 Done
56 Dish contents
57 Polynesian vegetable
58 Software buyer
59 Door frame
60 Done

10/39 Down repeated her role in the film version.

Marlo Thomas played 10/39 Down's role in the national tour.

The play was produced by the Lincoln Center Theater.

1	2	3	4	█	5	6	7	8	█	9	10	11	12	13
14				█	15				█	16				
17				█	18				█	19				
20				21					█	22				
23						█		24		█	█	█	█	█
25					█		26	27			█	28	29	30	31
█	█	█	█	32	33	34				█	35			
36	37	38	39	█	40					█	41			
42				█	43				44	█	█	█	█	█
45				█	46			█		47	48	49	50	51
█	█	█	52	53		█		54	55					
56	57	58			█	59	60							
61				█	62			█	63				
64				█	65			█	66				
67				█	68			█	69				

44 A STREETCAR NAMED DESIRE (1947)

"Whoever you are—I have always depended on the kindness of strangers."

ACROSS

1 From the U.S.
5 Lemon drinks
9 Like Havel
14 Unchanged
15 Long hair
16 Rental agreement
17 Conversation filler
18 Green-__ monster
19 Put on display
20 Star of the play
23 Byron, for one
24 Symbol of oppression
25 Prefix meaning "equal"
28 French lace
29 Kept
31 Half a Faulkner title
34 Reach
36 Germ-free
37 20 Across' role
42 Rose leaf
43 Wagner work
44 Snark's creator
47 Night-school course: Abbr.
48 Short putt
51 Poet Lowell
52 Chess piece
54 Destroy slowly
56 A star of the play
59 Jazz pianist Art
62 Duel prelude, perhaps
63 Main point
64 Abound
65 Just sitting around
66 Director Preminger
67 *Born Free* setting
68 Scaleless fish
69 Noble gas

DOWN

1 Foundation Trilogy author
2 Ancient Mideast fortress
3 TV chef
4 Is knocked for a loop
5 Solemn assent
6 *Godspell* tune
7 First month in Mexico
8 "Calendar Girl" singer
9 Dressed
10 Mr. Mostel
11 Musical ability
12 Civil War letters
13 "Wait a minute!"
21 Fictional Moor
22 Kan. neighbor
25 __ de la Société
26 Saturate
27 Prefix for present
30 Goddess of retribution
32 One of the Merry Men
33 __ breve
34 Snarl
35 Bout ender
37 Dog-license org.
38 Collaborators
39 Give it __ (go for it)
40 Wide-open audition
41 Director Craven
45 Yard-sale staples
46 Eric Knight title character
48 Marquee word
49 Augments
50 __ *Place*
53 *A Woman of No Importance* author
55 Tease
56 *12 Angry Men* group
57 Jane Austen book
58 Tailless simians
59 "For shame!"
60 Make humble
61 *The Bonesetter's Daughter* author

Other members of the original cast
included Kim Stanley and Karl Malden.

The play
was
originally
titled *The
Poker
Night.*

The play was produced by Irene
Selznick, daughter of Louis B. Mayer.

45 WENDY WASSERSTEIN

First play: *Any Woman Can't* (1973)

ACROSS

1 Pet-advocate org.
6 Warbled
10 Instance
14 Tennis star Monica
15 Genealogy diagram
16 Web-page visits
17 Be frugal
18 Petri-dish substance
19 Mars alias
20 With 57 Across, Wasserstein play
22 Philosopher Descartes
23 Mork's birthplace
24 *Bloodline* author
26 Eternally
29 Actress Lupino
32 Extremely, in slang
33 Fruit drink
35 Check the books
37 Chopin, to Sand
40 With *The*, Wasserstein play
43 Have to pay
44 Purple shade
45 Tariff-reducing treaty
46 __ and haw
47 *Guys and Dolls* character
49 Slothful
50 *The Human Comedy* author
54 *The Professor and the Madman* subject: Abbr.
56 List-ending abbreviation
57 See 20 Across
63 Pessimistic
64 Civil unrest
65 Author Lagerlöf
66 Adjutant
67 City on a fjord
68 *Romola* author
69 Aberdeen girl
70 Advertising sign
71 Quench

DOWN

1 Helper: Abbr.
2 Brother of Abel
3 Ballet bend
4 Emulated Cato
5 Buzzing
6 OR order
7 Lobby for
8 Closes in on
9 *Girl Crazy* composer
10 Film based on *Flowers for Algernon*
11 Made public
12 Courtroom worker
13 German city
21 Compete in the slalom
25 Like some kitchens
26 Lover of Narcissus
27 *A __ From the Bridge*
28 Singer Adams
30 Willy Wonka creator
31 New Age atmospheres
34 "Little Orphant Annie" writer
36 Berth
37 __ Romeo
38 French city
39 Londoner's exclamation
41 Ferber novel
42 *God's Little Acre* author
46 "Old Ironsides" poet
48 Thither partner
50 *Love Story* author
51 Skylit lobbies
52 Quantrill activities
53 Sleep disturber
55 Curved letters
58 By oneself
59 Harrow rival
60 Literary pseudonym
61 Half a self-help book title
62 Airport unit

40 Across won both a Pulitzer Prize and a Tony Award.

She received an under-graduate degree from Mount Holyoke and a master's degree from Yale.

The title characters of 20 Across were first portrayed by Jane Alexander, Madeline Kahn and Frances McDormand.

46 THE SUNSHINE BOYS (1972)

"I don't even want to discuss it. And in the second place, I would definitely not do it without a rehearsal."

ACROSS

1 *Inherit the Wind* lawyer
6 Little shavers
10 Bank customer: Abbr.
14 "A Visit From St. Nicholas" poet
15 Outspoken
16 Vientiane's country
17 Sommelier's stock
18 Spanish painter
19 Let fall
20 Comedy team in the play
23 United Nations Day month: Abbr.
24 Polyphemus had one
25 Actor who directed the play
30 On a cruise
35 "The Ransom of __ Chief"
36 Mann's refusal
37 Theater fare
38 Icelandic epic
40 *Golden Boy* character
42 Reply to the Little Red Hen
43 Sartre play
45 Construction girder
47 Senator Kennedy
48 Much of Chile
49 Original cast member of the play
51 *I __ Camera*
53 Linguistic suffix
54 Original cast member of the play
61 Medical thriller
62 Author Didion
63 Meat garnish
65 Put one's foot __
66 Prefix meaning "all"
67 Virginia Davis' stage name
68 Seven __ of man
69 *Ten Days That Shook the World* author
70 Pliny the __

DOWN

1 German export
2 Muddy up
3 First-class
4 Made use of
5 Sammy Davis Jr. autobiography
6 Sorenstam org.
7 Extremely long period
8 17th-century poet laureate
9 Actor Keach
10 *Guys and Dolls* original cast member
11 Gideon Fell creator
12 Author of 61 Across
13 Sugar amt.
21 Mason's aide
22 "The Owl and the Pussycat" poet
25 Gladiator's place
26 Enticed
27 Threw in
28 Barnyard baby
29 *Gunga Din* setting
31 Brown shade
32 Struck down
33 Consumed
34 Remark to the audience
37 Merchant
39 Lizzie Borden weapon
41 Apple competitor
44 Author Dinesen
46 Produce a revival
49 Biblical temptress
50 Watercraft
52 Significant
54 *Fear of Flying* author
55 Grenoble girlfriend
56 Lloyd Webber score
57 Calamity
58 Author Bagnold
59 Newspaper page
60 *The __ Tailors* (Sayers novel)
61 OSS successor
64 1 Down, for one

Neil Simon's inspiration was the
vaudeville team of Smith and Dale.

1	2	3	4	5		6	7	8	9		10	11	12	13
14						15					16			
17						18					19			
	20				21				22				
			23				24						
25	26	27			28	29			30	31	32	33	34
35				36				37					
38			39		40		41			42			
43				44			45			46		47	
48					49					50			
			51	52				53					
	54	55	56			57	58				59	60	
61				62				63					64
65				66				67					
68				69				70					

The 1997
Broadway
revival
starred
Jack
Klugman
and Tony
Randall.

This was Simon's follow-up to
The Prisoner of Second Avenue.

47 TOBACCO ROAD (1933)

"We got to stop cussing Him when we ain't got nothing to eat."

ACROSS

1 "The Tortoise and the Hare," e.g.
6 Queequeg's captain
10 Celeritous
14 Flynn of films
15 Parlor piece
16 General Bradley
17 *Peter Pan* staging need
18 Criticize
19 Lawn tool
20 Preacher in the play
23 Floppy-eared dog
26 Wall climber
27 Medieval instrument
28 Killer whale
32 Writer Calvino
36 Culture medium
37 Part of speech
38 *Beggerman,* __
39 Gist
40 Setting of the play
42 WWII fliers
43 Perry Mason's investigator
45 Laced up
46 Recording medium
47 __ Martin (007 auto)
48 Singer showcases
49 Champagne bucket
50 New Deal agcy.
52 Sports-team bosses
54 Character in the play
60 Overture follower
61 Like George Apley
62 Greek letters
66 Benedictine, e.g.
67 Biblical prophet
68 Agitates
69 __ B'rith
70 *Da* opposite
71 C sharp alias

DOWN

1 Not a lot
2 *Exodus* character
3 "It's cold!"
4 *How to Succeed in Business . . .* composer
5 __ *Venner* (Holmes novel)
6 Man Friday: Abbr.
7 Logical inconsistency
8 Worship from __
9 Felix Salten novel
10 *The Day of the Jackal* author
11 *Amo,* __, *amat*
12 Munro's pen name
13 Lemon or lime
21 *Lust for Life* author
22 Lloyd Webber score
23 Football great George
24 Soothsayers
25 __ *Mater*
29 "The Saga of an American Family"
30 *Objet d'art*
31 Heavenly messenger
33 Rickenbacker was one
34 Track athlete, at times
35 Proposals to buy
40 Literary category
41 Prince Myshkin
44 Heyerdahl book
46 End of a Tennessee Williams title
51 *Bloomer Girl* composer
53 Peculiar
54 Window frame
55 Nobel Prize category: Abbr.
56 Sicilian volcano
57 Do-nothing
58 To be: Fr.
59 Bike part
63 Shortened preposition
64 __ carte
65 Former Air France plane

The play was written by Jack Kirkland,
based on Erskine Caldwell's novel.

It ran for
3,182
perfor-
mances
in its
original
Broadway
run.

It opened on the last night of
Prohibition.

48 WAITING FOR GODOT (1953)

"We are all born mad. Some remain so."

ACROSS

1 California peak
7 Campaign nickname of '36
10 Nigeria neighbor
14 Conqueror of Mexico
15 Crossword-clue abbreviation
16 Give up
17 Not completely
18 __ Amin
19 Film role for Shirley
20 "That's amazing!"
21 He's waiting for Godot
23 *Exit the King* author
27 Mess up
28 Weapon
29 Goddess of the hunt
30 Rice alternative
32 Originally called
33 *M*A*S*H* star
34 Keyboard key
35 *The Faerie Queen* character
37 Author of the play
42 Long ago, in poems
43 Where Mindy honeymooned
44 Earring style
46 14 Across quest
49 Greek letter

51 __ boom
52 Boiling
53 Capek play
54 *Oliver's Story* and *Twenty Years After*
56 He's waiting for Godot
59 *Manhattan Transfer* character
60 Annual basketball tourney
61 Dash off
62 Whine
66 Set-tos
67 *Foucault's Pendulum* author
68 Laud
69 Slangy assent
70 Japanese honorific
71 Saw to

DOWN

1 __-fi
2 Darling
3 Klee colleague
4 Performer's alias
5 Spanish saint
6 14 Across victim
7 Tel __
8 Soup servers
9 Robin Hood cohort

10 10% of MMXX
11 Ishmael's creator
12 Look up to
13 Ustinov autobiography
22 Imbibed
23 Muckraker Tarbell
24 Stops from squeaking
25 Zilch
26 Whitish gem
31 Church official
34 Sylvia Plath's husband
36 *A Shropshire Lad* poet
38 Prefix for violet
39 Chapters of history
40 Literary mood
41 Slave away
45 Apple alternatives
46 "The Last Leaf" author
47 Gat
48 Parliament city
50 Beethoven symphony
51 Nerdish
55 Exodus setting
57 Too hurried
58 Light gas
63 Stream starter
64 Compass pt.
65 Bolshevik

21 Across' nickname is Didi.

56 Across' nickname is Gogo.

Pozzo and Lucky are master and slave.

49 WHO'S AFRAID OF VIRGINIA WOOLF? (1962)

"I hope that was an empty bottle. . . . You can't afford to waste good liquor, not on your salary!"

ACROSS

1 Tinseltown force: Abbr.
5 Wine containers
9 *Conning Tower* columnist
14 Rights org.
15 Orchestral instrument
16 Victor of 1917
17 French designer
18 Jungle sound
19 Middle Easterner
20 Author of the play
23 Helpful hint
24 Unmixed
25 *Paradise Lost* character
27 Derived from milk
30 '60s novelty dance
35 Mess up
36 Improve, as skills
38 Attain
39 Main characters of the play
43 Bring on
44 '50s Congressional grp.
45 Female lobster
46 Genteel
48 Dr. Jekyll's alter ego
51 Get the point
52 Two-way
53 Three-time boxing champ

56 Setting of the play
62 Reformer Riis
64 Talk wildly
65 Manipulative sort
66 *The Jungle Book* wolf
67 Rich Little, for one
68 *The Old Curiosity Shop* girl
69 "I Am Woman" singer
70 Bouquet
71 Alison Lurie novel surname

DOWN

1 Take on cargo
2 Corrosive chemical
3 *Speed-the-__*
4 *The Age of Napoleon* author
5 *Rich Man, Poor Man* family name
6 WWII battleship target
7 Aspiration
8 Citizen of Sarajevo
9 Ointment ingredient
10 FDR or JFK
11 Med.-school course
12 Short skirt
13 Make a cut
21 Defendants, in law
22 Moray

26 One watching
27 Kosher
28 Basketball stadium
29 Nile beasts
30 Negate
31 Mother of Castor
32 Cartoonist Guisewite
33 Needed liniment
34 Macbeth title
37 Maui neighbor
40 Furrows
41 Wisconsin city
42 *Lonesome Dove* author
47 Agent's cut, e.g.
49 Pied Piper follower
50 Texas oilman
52 Hans Christian Andersen et al.
53 Not fully closed
54 __ Poets (Coleridge and colleagues)
55 Guaranteed
57 Prepare a present
58 Guitar device
59 Between ports
60 Moolah
61 __ Stanley Gardner
63 Like Mother Hubbard

Arthur Hill and Uta Hagen originated
the characters of 39 Across on
Broadway.

1	2	3	4	■	5	6	7	8	■	9	10	11	12	13
14				■	15				■	16				
17				■	18				■	19				
20				21				22		■	23			
■	■		24			■	■	25		26	■	■	■	■
27	28	29			■	30	31			■	32	33	34
35			■	■	36	37			■	38			
39			40	41				42					
43				■	44			■	■	45			
46				47			■	48	49	50			
■	■	51			■	52				■	■	■
53	54	55	■	56		57	58				59	60	61
62			63		■	64			■	65			
66					■	67			■	68			
69					■	70			■	71			

20 Across
got the
title from
Greenwich
Village
graffiti.

The play won five Tony Awards.

50 TENNESSEE WILLIAMS

First play: *Cairo, Shanghai, Bombay* (1937)

ACROSS

1 *Artist in Crime* author
6 Louver part
10 904, to Nero
14 Government security
15 __ *Ado About Nothing*
16 Pasternak character
17 Williams play
19 Turow memoir
20 Ballet movement
21 Robert Lawrence __
22 "Let It Be Forgotten" poet
27 Sweater material
28 Pleads a case
29 Du Maurier novel
30 Long feather
31 Feudal workers
33 Ore layer
34 Formal dances
35 Eschew food
39 In a weird way
41 Bar mitzvah reading
42 Walter Mitty creator
45 *Terms of Endearment* character
46 *Interview* magazine founder
47 Kipling subject
49 Welles of filmdom
50 Org. once headed by Eisenhower
51 __ *accompli*
52 Williams play
58 Seabird
59 Crude cartel
60 Object of Ahab's fixation
61 Teeter
62 *Skylab* org.
63 Seuss character

DOWN

1 VH1 alternative
2 Black cuckoo
3 Fish eggs
4 R followers
5 Witch's curse
6 Kemelman's rabbi
7 *Imaginary Friends* author
8 Land unit
9 Definite article
10 With 25 Down, Williams play
11 Wild man
12 Peaceful
13 Eamon De __
18 Ledger experts
21 __ it (amen)
22 Bugle call
23 Agatha contemporary
24 Water, to Juan
25 See 10 Down
26 Poor grade
27 Computer storage amounts, for short
29 Depend (on)
31 Sanctuary
32 Not well
34 *Jacques __ Is Alive and Well . . .*
36 Baseball superstar's nickname
37 Dress of India
38 Compared to
40 Deep black
41 Harbor boat
42 Theater discount ticket
43 Capital of Zimbabwe
44 Like Fuzzy-Wuzzy
45 Unattributed: Abbr.
47 Fun partner
48 New York city
50 California county
52 Opposed to
53 Symbol of Athena
54 Greek letter
55 Cup handle
56 In the style of
57 Superman foe Luthor

His given names are Thomas Lanier.

He received Kennedy Center Honors in 1979.

He received an honorary degree from Harvard in 1982.

MORE GREAT TITLES FROM STANLEY NEWMAN

VOL.	ISBN	QUAN.	PRICE	TOTAL

BY STANLEY NEWMAN

Stanley Newman's Cartoon Crosswords
0812934709 ___ $7.95 ___

Stanley Newman's Coffee Time Word Games
0812934539 ___ $7.95 ___

Random House Golf Crosswords
0812933966 ___ $7.95 ___

Stanley Newman's Literary Crosswords: Something Novel
0812935047 ___ $8.95 ___

Stanley Newman's Movie Mania Crosswords
0812934687 ___ $7.95 ___

Stanley Newman's Sitcom Crosswords,
0812934695 ___ $7.95 ___

New York Times Square One Crossword Puzzle Dictionary
by Stanley Newman and Daniel Stark
0812930436 ___ $23.00 ___

Stanley Newman's Ultimate Trivia Crosswords
Vol. 1 0812935160 ___ $9.95 ___

10,000 Answers: The Ultimate Trivia Encyclopedia
by Stanley Newman and Hal Fittipaldi
037571944X ___ $24.95 ___

EDITED BY STANLEY NEWMAN

Stanley Newman's Sunday Crosswords
Vol. 1 0812934512 ___ $9.95 ___
Vol. 2 0812935144 ___ $9.95 ___

Random House Back to the Beach Crosswords
0812934768 ___ $6.95 ___

Random House Bedtime Crosswords
0812934679 ___ $6.95 ___

Random House By the Fireside Crosswords
0812934199 ___ $6.95 ___

VOL.	ISBN	QUAN.	PRICE	TOTAL

Random House Cabin Fever Crosswords
0812934776 ___ $6.95 ___

Random House Cozy Crosswords
0812934326 ___ $6.95 ___

Random House Spring Training Crosswords
0812934784 ___ $6.95 ___

Random House Summer Vacation Crosswords
0812934792 ___ $6.95 ___

Random House Vacation Crosswords
0812932897 ___ $6.95 ___

Random House More Vacation Crosswords
0812934180 ___ $6.95 ___

Stanley Newman Cranium Crackers
0812934806 ___ $6.95 ___

Random House Club Crosswords
Edited by Stanley Newman and Mel Rosen
Vol. 1 0812926382 ___ $13.95 ___
Vol. 2 081292892X ___ $13.95 ___
Vol. 3 0812929691 ___ $13.95 ___

Random House Sunday Crosswords
Vol. 1 0812925548 ___ $9.95 ___

Random House Sunday Crossword Omnibus
Vol. 1 0812933982 ___ $12.95 ___

Random House Monster Sunday Crossword Omnibus
Vol. 1 0812930592 ___ $17.50 ___

Random House Monster Crossword Puzzle Omnibus
Vol. 1 0812932137 ___ $17.50 ___

Random House Mammoth Crossword Puzzle Omnibus
081293394X ___ $16.95 ___

Random House UltraHard Crossword Omnibus
Vol. 1 0812931262 ___ $12.50 ___

Random House Masterpiece Crosswords Collection
0812934946 ___ $12.95 ___

ANSWERS

1

```
URN   TRACT   GRIMM
NEE   ROLLO   ROTOR
IVE   EATEN   OPART
TEDDYROOSEVELT
ARLISS   IDE   III
SEED   ACLU   DAMS
      ESME  CORNEA
BROOKLYNNEWYORK
LOUNGE   TIDE
ASTO   URSA   VETS
HER   UTE   ETHNIC
MARTHABREWSTER
SAGET   DEERE   IDI
IRENE   ELSIE   RIB
RYDER   RATED   ENE
```

2

```
EDITOR   MCMAHON
CARBINE  CHORALE
DREAMER  MOSEYED
SPIRITUALISM
   NONE   RHYMES
TOBAGO  OSSA   EVE
EREI  NANA  RADII
MILDRED  NATWICK
PEASE  ABEL  ONTO
UNI  HUME  ACLASS
STREEP   ANNA
MADAMEARCATI
LIBERAL  PLEASED
TRIESTE  ADELINE
DECREES  LARIAT
```

3

```
BEANS  ECHO  NOBS
BLOOM  DRAW  ELLA
BILLIEDAWN  WEAN
   LLAMA   IRONY
STAGED   IONESCO
INLAY   PHILIP
TOUR  CEO  STUART
ATMS  HASTE  BRER
RESOLE  EEN  LENA
   NEVADA   SINAI
HAWKEYE   BACALL
AREAS   REALM
IMAN   HARRYBROCK
LEVI  ETAT  ACTII
EDEN  NESS  SATAN
```

4

```
STALK  FIRMS  ROT
WOMEN  ISAAC  ERA
AROSE  EAGLE  SIT
GERALDLYMAN  TET
   GLAD   OREGANO
JAKE  TIPPI  AUTO
ALI  DANL  ABBR
BAMBI  GAD  BEARD
   SEED  TUBS  NEE
AGTS  ECOLE  ETON
BEATSME   CLOD
BIN  WILLIAMINGE
ESL  ALLEN  ATOLL
SEE  PLANE  HOTEL
SLY  SERTA  ARENA
```

5

```
GUAM  WHOM  AFIRE
ONLY  HOPE  PAPER
ALOE  APER  AMONG
TINYALICE  CASTS
STEELE   MEN
   TROUPE   DABS
BOFFO  WHET  YULE
ODORS  NAP  HARTE
LIRA  ZEUS  AMASS
ONEG   ADLIBS
   MPG   UTOPIA
HOMER  LISTENING
ARENA  ABIT  TEEN
NATTY  NINE  ACRE
GLASS  EDER  PETS
```

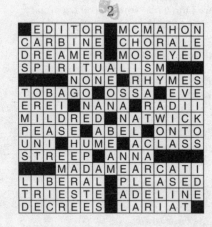

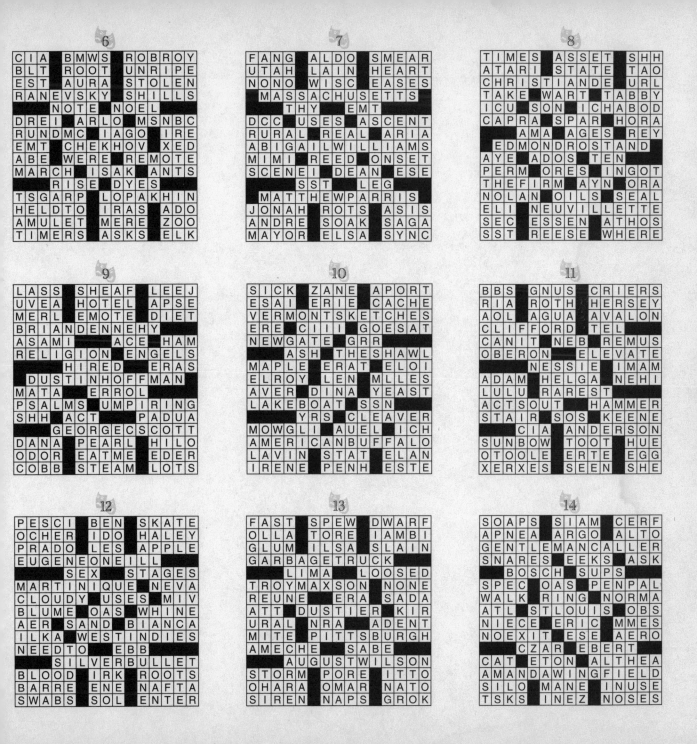

6

```
CIA  BMWS   ROBROY
BLT  ROOT   UNRIPE
EST  AURA   STOLEN
RANEVSKY   SHILLS
     NOTE  NOEL
DREI  ARLO  MSNBC
RUNDMC IAGO  IRE
EMT  CHEKHOV XED
ABE  WERE  REMOTE
MARCH ISAK  ANTS
      RISE DYES
TSGARP  LOPAKHIN
HELDTO IRAS  ADO
AMULET MERE  ZOO
TIMERS ASKS  ELK
```

7

```
FANG  ALDO  SMEAR
UTAH  LAIN  HEART
NONO  WISC  EASES
   MASSACHUSETTS
      THY  EMT
DCC  USES  ASCENT
RURAL REAL  ARIA
ABIGAILWILLIAMS
MIMI  REED  ONSET
SCENEI DEAN  ESE
       SST  LEG
  MATTHEWPARRIS
JONAH ROTS  ASIS
ANDRE SOAK  SAGA
MAYOR ELSA  SYNC
```

8

```
TIMES ASSET  SHH
ATARI STATE  TAO
CHRISTIANDE  URL
TAKE  WART  TABBY
ICU  SON  ICHABOD
      AMA AGES REY
 EDMONDROSTAND
AYE  ADOS   TEN
PERM  ORES INGOT
THEFIRM AYN  ORA
NOLAN OILS  SEAL
ELI  NEUVILLETTE
SEC  ESSEN ATHOS
SST  REESE WHERE
```

9

```
LASS  SHEAF  LEEJ
UVEA  HOTEL  APSE
MERL  EMOTE  DIET
BRIANDENNEHY
ASAMI   ACE   HAM
RELIGION  ENGELS
   HIRED   ERAS
  DUSTINHOFFMAN
MATA   ERROL
PSALMS  UMPIRING
SHH  ACT   PADUA
  GEORGECSCOTT
DANA  PEARL  HILO
ODOR  EATME  EDER
COBB  STEAM  LOTS
```

10

```
SICK  ZANE  APORT
ESAI  ERIE  CACHE
VERMONTSKETCHES
ERE  CIII  GOESAT
NEWGATE   GRR
   ASH  THESHAWL
MAPLE  ERAT  ELOI
ELROY  LEN  MLLES
AVER  DINA  YEAST
LAKEBOAT   SSN
   YRS  CLEAVER
MOWGLI AUEL  ICH
AMERICANBUFFALO
LAVIN STAT  ELAN
IRENE PENH  ESTE
```

11

```
BBS  GNUS  CRIERS
RIA  ROTH  HERSEY
AOL  AGUA  AVALON
CLIFFORD   TEL
CANIT  NEB  REMUS
OBERON  ELEVATE
     NESSIE  IMAM
ADAM  HELGA  NEHI
LULU  RAREST
ACTSOUT  HAMMER
STAIR SOS  KEENE
     CIA ANDERSON
SUNBOW TOOT  HUE
OTOOLE ERTE  EGG
XERXES SEEN  SHE
```

12

```
PESCI  BEN  SKATE
OCHER  IDO  HALEY
PRADO  LES  APPLE
EUGENEONEILL
   SEX   STAGES
MARTINIQUE  NEVA
CLOUDY USES  MIV
BLUME  OAS  WHINE
AER  SAND  BIANCA
ILKA  WESTINDIES
NEEDTO   EBB
  SILVERBULLET
BLOOD  IRK  ROOTS
BARRE  ENE  NAFTA
SWABS  SOL  ENTER
```

13

```
FAST  SPEW  DWARF
OLLA  TORE  IAMBI
GLUM  ILSA  SLAIN
GARBAGETRUCK
   LIMA   LOOSED
TROYMAXSON  NONE
REUNE  ERA  SADA
ATT  DUSTIER  KIR
URAL  NRA  ADENT
MITE  PITTSBURGH
AMECHE  SABE
  AUGUSTWILSON
STORM  PORE  ITTO
OHARA  OMAR  NATO
SIREN  NAPS  GROK
```

14

```
SOAPS  SIAM  CERF
APNEA  ARGO  ALTO
GENTLEMANCALLER
SNARES EEKS  ASK
   BOSCH   SUPS
SPEC  OAS  PENPAL
WALK  RING  NORMA
ATL  STLOUIS  OBS
NIECE ERIC  MMES
NOEXIT ESE  AERO
     CZAR  EBERT
CAT  ETON  ALTHEA
AMANDAWINGFIELD
SILO  MANE  INUSE
TSKS  INEZ  NOSES
```

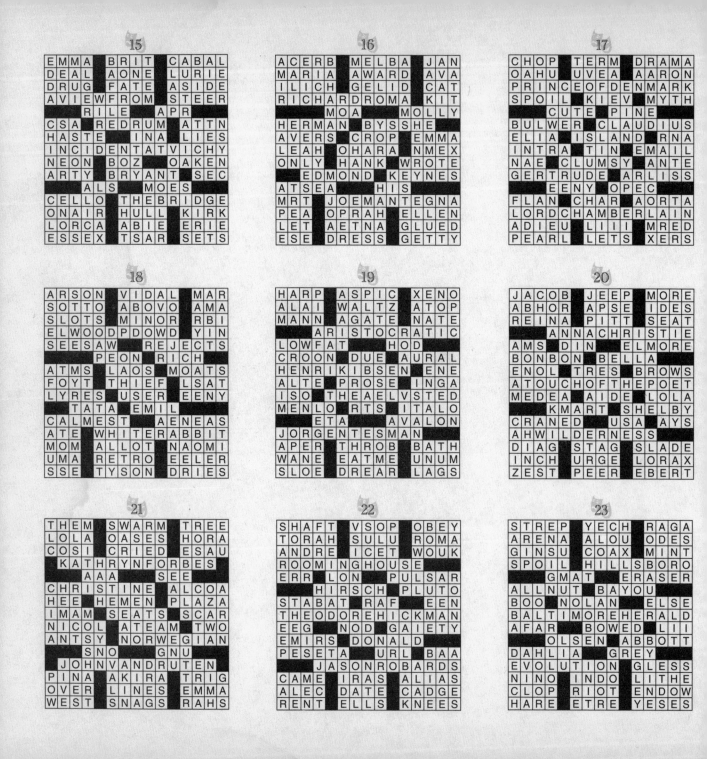

15

```
EMMA . BRIT . CABAL
DEAL . AONE . LURIE
DRUG . FATE . ASIDE
AVIEWFROM . STEER
. . RILE . . APR .
CSA . REDRUM . ATTN
HASTE . INA . LIES
INCIDENTATVICHY
NEON . BOZ . OAKEN
ARTY . BRYANT . SEC
. . ALS . . MOES .
CELLO . THEBRIDGE
ONAIR . HULL . KIRK
LORCA . ABIE . ERIE
ESSEX . TSAR . SETS
```

16

```
ACERB . MELBA . JAN
MARIA . AWARD . AVA
ILICH . GELID . CAT
RICHARDROMA . KIT
. . . MOA . MOLLY
HERMAN . BYSSHE
AVERS . CROP . EMMA
LEAH . OHARA . NMEX
ONLY . HANK . WROTE
. EDMOND . KEYNES
ATSEA . HIS . . .
MRT . JOEMANTEGNA
PEA . OPRAH . ELLEN
LET . AETNA . GLUED
ESE . DRESS . GETTY
```

17

```
CHOP . TERM . DRAMA
OAHU . UVEA . AARON
PRINCEOFDENMARK
SPOIL . KIEV . MYTH
. . CUTE . PINE . .
BULWER . CLAUDIUS
ELIA . ISLAND . RNA
INTRA . TIN . EMAIL
NAE . CLUMSY . ANTE
GERTRUDE . ARLISS
. . EENY . OPEC . .
FLAN . CHAR . AORTA
LORDCHAMBERLAIN
ADIEU . LIII . MRED
PEARL . LETS . XERS
```

18

```
ARSON . VIDAL . MAR
SOTTO . ABOVO . AMA
SLOTS . MINOR . RBI
ELWOODPDOWD . YIN
SEESAW . REJECTS
. . PEON . RICH . .
ATMS . LAOS . MOATS
FOYT . THIEF . LSAT
LYRES . USER . EENY
. TATA . EMIL . .
CALMEST . AENEAS
ATE . WHITERABBIT
MOM . ALLOT . NAOMI
UMA . RETRO . EELER
SSE . TYSON . DRIES
```

19

```
HARP . ASPIC . XENO
ALAI . WALTZ . ATOP
MANN . AGATE . NATE
. ARISTOCRATIC
LOWFAT . HOD . .
CROON . DUE . AURAL
HENRIKIBSEN . ENE
ALTE . PROSE . INGA
ISO . THEAELVSTED
MENLO . RTS . ITALO
. ETA . AVALON .
JORGENTESMAN
APER . THROB . BATH
WANE . EATME . UNUM
SLOE . DREAR . LAGS
```

20

```
JACOB . JEEP . MORE
ABHOR . APSE . IDES
REINA . PITT . SEAT
. ANNACHRISTIE
AMS . DIN . ELMORE
BONBON . BELLA .
ENOL . TRES . BROWS
ATOUCHOFTHEPOET
MEDEA . AIDE . LOLA
. KMART . SHELBY
CRANED . USA . AYS
AHWILDERNESS
DIAG . STAG . SLADE
INCH . URGE . LORAX
ZEST . PEER . EBERT
```

21

```
THEM . SWARM . TREE
LOLA . OASES . HORA
COSI . CRIED . ESAU
. KATHRYNFORBES .
. . AAA . . SEE .
CHRISTINE . ALCOA
HEE . HEMEN . PLAZA
IMAM . SEATS . SCAR
NICOL . ATEAM . TWO
ANTSY . NORWEGIAN
. . SNO . . GNU .
. JOHNVANDRUTEN .
PINA . AKIRA . TRIG
OVER . LINES . EMMA
WEST . SNAGS . RAHS
```

22

```
SHAFT . VSOP . OBEY
TORAH . SULU . ROMA
ANDRE . ICET . WOUK
ROOMINGHOUSE .
ERR . LON . PULSAR
. HIRSCH . PLUTO
STABAT . RAF . EEN
THEODOREHICKMAN
EEG . NOD . GAIETY
EMIRS . DONALD .
PESETA . URL . BAA
. JASONROBARDS
CAME . IRAS . ALIAS
ALEC . DATE . CADGE
RENT . ELLS . KNEES
```

23

```
STREP . YECH . RAGA
ARENA . ALOU . ODES
GINSU . COAX . MINT
SPOIL . HILLSBORO
. GMAT . ERASER
ALLNUT . BAYOU
BOO . NOLAN . ELSE
BALTIMOREHERALD
AFAR . BOWED . LII
. OLSEN . ABBOTT
DAHLIA . GREY .
EVOLUTION . GLESS
NINO . INDO . LITHE
CLOP . RIOT . ENDOW
HARE . ETRE . YESES
```

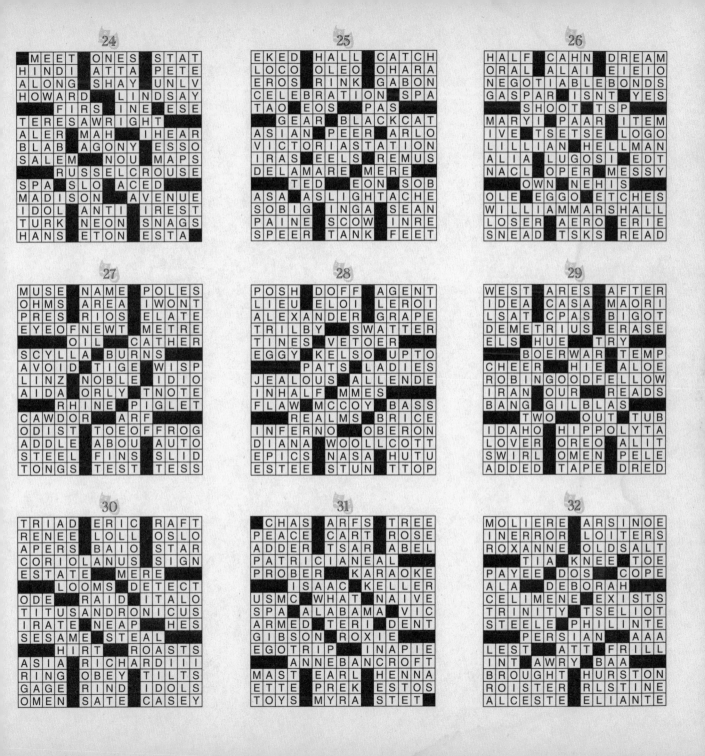

24

```
MEET  ONES   STAT
HINDI ATTA   PETE
ALONG SHAY   UNLV
HOWARD  LINDSAY
   FIRS INE ESE
TERESAWRIGHT
ALER  MAH  IHEAR
BLAB AGONY  ESSO
SALEM  NOU  MAPS
  RUSSELCROUSE
SPA  SLO   ACED
MADISON  AVENUE
IDOL ANTI  IREST
TURK NEON  SNAGS
HANS ETON   ESTA
```

25

```
EKED  HALL   CATCH
LOCO  OLEO   OHARA
EROS  RINK   GABON
CELEBRATION   SPA
TAO  EOS    PAS
  GEAR  BLACKCAT
ASIAN  PEER  ARLO
VICTORIASTATION
IRAS  EELS  REMUS
DELAMARE   MERE
   TED EON  SOB
ASA  ASLIGHTACHE
SOBIG INGA   SEAN
PAINE SCOW   INRE
SPEER TANK   FEET
```

26

```
HALF  CAHN   DREAM
ORAL  ALAI   EIEIO
NEGOTIABLEBONDS
GASPAR  ISNT  YES
   SHOOT  TSP
MARYI  PAAR  ITEM
IVE  TSETSE  LOGO
LILLIAN  HELLMAN
ALIA  LUGOSI  EDT
NACL  OPER  MESSY
   OWN  NEHIS
OLE  EGGO  ETCHES
WILLIAMMARSHALL
LOSER  AERO  ERIE
SNEAD  TSKS  READ
```

27

```
MUSE  NAME   POLES
OHMS  AREA   IWONT
PRES  RIOS   ELATE
EYEOFNEWT   METRE
    OIL  CATHER
SCYLLA   BURNS
AVOID  TIGE  WISP
LINZ  NOBLE  IDIO
AIDA  ORLY  TNOTE
  RHINE  PIGLET
CAWDOR   ARF
ODIST  TOEOFFROG
ADDLE  ABOU  AUTO
STEEL  FINS  SLID
TONGS  TEST  TESS
```

28

```
POSH  DOFF   AGENT
LIEU  ELOI   LEROI
ALEXANDER   GRAPE
TRILBY   SWATTER
TINES  VETOER
EGGY  KELSO  UPTO
   PATS  LADIES
JEALOUS  ALLENDE
INHALF   MMES
FLAW  MCCOY  BASS
  REALMS  BRICE
INFERNO   OBERON
DIANA  WOOLLCOTT
EPICS  NASA  HUTU
ESTEE  STUN  TTOP
```

29

```
WEST  ARES   AFTER
IDEA  CASA   MAORI
LSAT  CPAS   BIGOT
DEMETRIUS   ERASE
ELS  HUE    TRY
  BOERWAR   TEMP
CHEER  HIE  ALOE
ROBINGOODFELLOW
IRAN  OUR   READS
BANG  GILBLAS
  TWO  OUT  TUB
IDAHO  HIPPOLYTA
LOVER  OREO  ALIT
SWIRL  OMEN  PELE
ADDED  TAPE  DRED
```

30

```
TRIAD  ERIC   RAFT
RENEE  LOLL   OSLO
APERS  BAIO   STAR
CORIOLANUS   SIGN
ESTATE   MERE
  LOOMS  DETECT
ODE  RAID  ITALO
TITUSANDRONICUS
IRATE  NEAP  HES
SESAME   STEAL
  HIRT  ROASTS
ASIA  RICHARDIII
RING  OBEY  TILTS
GAGE  RIND  IDOLS
OMEN  SATE  CASEY
```

31

```
 CHAS  ARFS   TREE
PEACE  CART   ROSE
ADDER  TSAR   ABEL
PATRICIANEAL
PROBER   KARAOKE
  ISAAC  KELLER
USMC  WHAT  NAIVE
SPA  ALABAMA  VIC
ARMED  TERI  DENT
GIBSON  ROXIE
EGOTRIP   INAPIE
ANNEBANCROFT
MAST  EARL  HENNA
ETTE  PREK  ESTOS
TOYS  MYRA  STET
```

32

```
MOLIERE   ARSINOE
INERROR   LOITERS
ROXANNE   OLDSALT
  TIA  KNEE  TOE
PAYEE  DOS   COPE
ALA  DEBORAH
CELIMENE   EXISTS
TRINITY   TSELIOT
STEELE   PHILINTE
  PERSIAN   AAA
LEST  ATT  FRILL
INT  AWRY   BAA
BROUGHT   HURSTON
ROISTER   RLSTINE
ALCESTE   ELIANTE
```

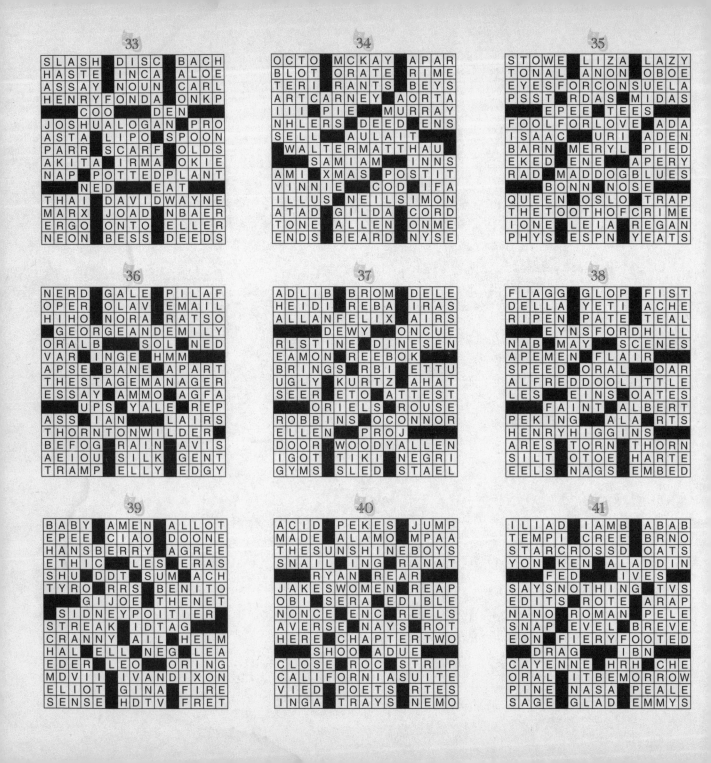

33

```
SLASH DISC BACH
HASTE INCA ALOE
ASSAY NOUN CARL
HENRYFONDA ONKP
    COO    DEN
JOSHUALOGAN PRO
ASTA LIPO SPOON
PARR SCARF OLDS
AKITA IRMA OKIE
NAP POTTEDPLANT
    NED    EAT
THAI DAVIDWAYNE
MARX JOAD NBAER
ERGO ONTO ELLER
NEON BESS DEEDS
```

34

```
OCTO MCKAY APAR
BLOT ORATE RIME
TERI RANTS BEYS
ARTCARNEY AORTA
IIII PIE MURRAY
NHLERS DEED ENS
SELL AULAIT
WALTERMATTHAU
SAMIAM INNS
AMI XMAS POSTIT
VINNIE COD IFA
ILLUS NEILSIMON
ATAD GILDA CORD
TONE ALLEN ONME
ENDS BEARD NYSE
```

35

```
STOWE LIZA LAZY
TONAL ANON OBOE
EYESFORCONSUELA
PSST RDAS MIDAS
    EPEE TEES
FOOLFORLOVE ADA
ISAAC URI ADEN
BARN MERYL PIED
EKED ENE APERY
RAD MADDOGBLUES
    BONN NOSE
QUEEN OSLO TRAP
THETOOTHOFCRIME
IONE LEIA REGAN
PHYS ESPN YEATS
```

36

```
NERD GALE PILAF
OPER OLAV EMAIL
HIHO NORA RATSO
GEORGEANDEMILY
ORALB SOL NED
VAR INGE HMM
APSE BANE APART
THESTAGEMANAGER
ESSAY AMMO AGFA
UPS YALE REP
ASS IAN LAIRS
THORNTONWILDER
BEFOG RAIN AVIS
AEIOU SILK GENT
TRAMP ELLY EDGY
```

37

```
ADLIB BROM DELE
HEIDI REBA IRAS
ALLANFELIX AIRS
    DEWY ONCUE
RLSTINE DINESEN
EAMON REEBOK
BRINGS RBI ETTU
UGLY KURTZ AHAT
SEER ETO ATTEST
    ORIELS ROUSE
ROBBINS OCONNOR
ELLEN PROJ
DOOR WOODYALLEN
IGOT TIKI NEGRI
GYMS SLED STAEL
```

38

```
FLAGG GLOP FIST
DELLA YETI ACHE
RIPEN PATE TEAL
EYNSFORDHILL
NAB MAY SCENES
APEMEN FLAIR
SPEED ORAL OAR
ALFREDDOOLITTLE
LES EINS OATES
FAINT ALBERT
PEKING ALA RTS
HENRYHIGGINS
ARES TORN THORN
SILT OTOE HARTE
EELS NAGS EMBED
```

39

```
BABY AMEN ALLOT
EPEE CIAO DOONE
HANSBERRY AGREE
ETHIC LES ERAS
SHU DDT SUM ACH
TYRO RRS BENITO
GIJOE THENET
SIDNEYPOITIER
STREAK IDTAG
CRANNY AIL HELM
HAL ELL NEG LEA
EDER LEO ORING
MDVII IVANDIXON
ELIOT GINA FIRE
SENSE HDTV FRET
```

40

```
ACID PEKES JUMP
MADE ALAMO MPAA
THESUNSHINEBOYS
SNAIL ING RANAT
    RYAN REAR
JAKESWOMEN REAP
OBI SERA EDIBLE
NONCE ENC REELS
AVERSE NAYS ROT
HERE CHAPTERTWO
    SHOO ADUE
CLOSE ROC STRIP
CALIFORNIASUITE
VIED POETS RTES
INGA TRAYS NEMO
```

41

```
ILIAD IAMB ABAB
TEMPI CREE BRNO
STARCROSSD OATS
YON KEN ALADDIN
    FED    IVES
SAYSNOTHING TVS
EDITS ROTE ARAP
NANO ROMAN PELE
SNAP EVEL BREVE
EON FIERYFOOTED
    DRAG    IBN
CAYENNE HRH CHE
ORAL ITBEMORROW
PINE NASA PEALE
SAGE GLAD EMMYS
```

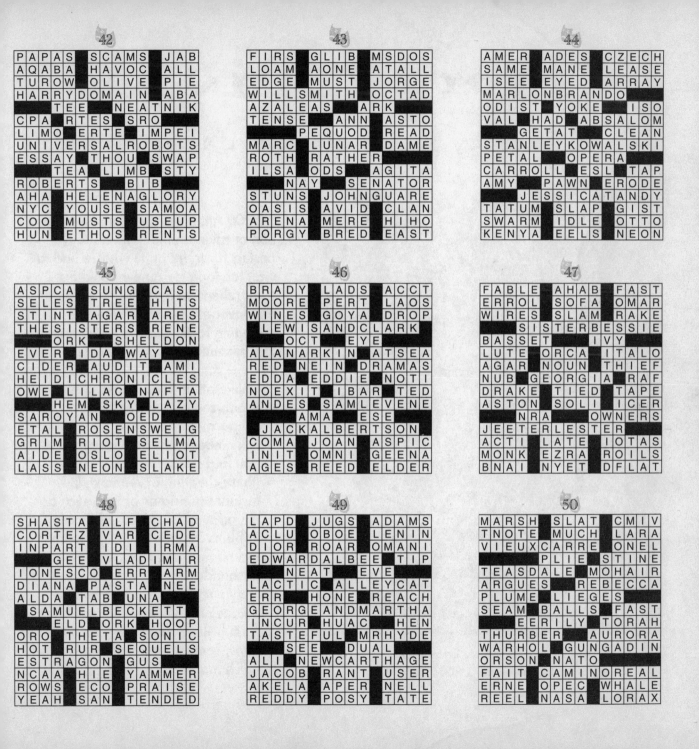

42

```
PAPAS SCAMS JAB
AQABA HAVOC ALL
TUROW OLIVE PIE
HARRYDOMAIN ABA
     TEE NEATNIK
CPA RTES    SRO
LIMO ERTE IMPEI
UNIVERSALROBOTS
ESSAY THOU SWAP
   TEA LIMB STY
ROBERTS    BIB
AHA HELENAGLORY
NYC YOUSE SAMOA
COO MUSTS USEUP
HUN ETHOS RENTS
```

43

```
FIRS GLIB MSDOS
LOAM AONE ATALL
EDGE MUST JORGE
WILLSMITH OCTAD
AZALEAS    ARK
TENSE ANN  ASTO
     PEQUOD READ
MARC LUNAR DAME
ROTH RATHER
ILSA ODS   AGITA
     NAY SENATOR
STUNS JOHNGUARE
OASIS AVID CLAN
ARENA MERE HIHO
PORGY BRED EAST
```

44

```
AMER ADES CZECH
SAME MANE LEASE
ISEE EYED ARRAY
MARLONBRANDO
ODIST YOKE   ISO
VAL HAD ABSALOM
    GETAT  CLEAN
STANLEYKOWALSKI
PETAL    OPERA
CARROLL ESL TAP
AMY PAWN  ERODE
    JESSICATANDY
TATUM SLAP GIST
SWARM IDLE OTTO
KENYA EELS NEON
```

45

```
ASPCA SUNG CASE
SELES TREE HITS
STINT AGAR ARES
THESISTERS RENE
   ORK SHELDON
EVER IDA WAY
CIDER AUDIT AMI
HEIDICHRONICLES
OWE LILAC NAFTA
   HEM SKY LAZY
SAROYAN    OED
ETAL ROSENSWEIG
GRIM RIOT SELMA
AIDE OSLO ELIOT
LASS NEON SLAKE
```

46

```
BRADY LADS ACCT
MOORE PERT LAOS
WINES GOYA DROP
 LEWISANDCLARK
   OCT    EYE
ALANARKIN ATSEA
RED NEIN DRAMAS
EDDA EDDIE NOTI
NOEXIT IBAR TED
ANDES SAMLEVENE
    AMA   ESE
 JACKALBERTSON
COMA JOAN ASPIC
INIT OMNI GEENA
AGES REED ELDER
```

47

```
FABLE AHAB FAST
ERROL SOFA OMAR
WIRES SLAM RAKE
   SISTERBESSIE
BASSET    IVY
LUTE ORCA ITALO
AGAR NOUN THIEF
NUB GEORGIA RAF
DRAKE TIED TAPE
ASTON SOLI ICER
    NRA  OWNERS
JEETERLESTER
ACTI LATE IOTAS
MONK EZRA ROILS
BNAI NYET DFLAT
```

48

```
SHASTA ALF CHAD
CORTEZ VAR CEDE
INPART IDI IRMA
   GEE VLADIMIR
IONESCO ERR ARM
DIANA PASTA NEE
ALDA TAB UNA
 SAMUELBECKETT
   ELD ORK HOOP
ORO THETA SONIC
HOT RUR SEQUELS
ESTRAGON   GUS
NCAA HIE YAMMER
ROWS ECO PRAISE
YEAH SAN TENDED
```

49

```
LAPD JUGS ADAMS
ACLU OBOE LENIN
DIOR ROAR OMANI
EDWARDALBEE TIP
   NEAT    EVE
LACTIC ALLEYCAT
ERR HONE  REACH
GEORGEANDMARTHA
INCUR HUAC HEN
TASTEFUL MRHYDE
    SEE  DUAL
ALI NEWCARTHAGE
JACOB RANT USER
AKELA APER NELL
REDDY POSY TATE
```

50

```
MARSH SLAT CMIV
TNOTE MUCH LARA
VIEUXCARRE ONEL
     PLIE STINE
TEASDALE MOHAIR
ARGUES  REBECCA
PLUME LIEGES
SEAM BALLS FAST
   EERILY TORAH
THURBER AURORA
WARHOL GUNGADIN
ORSON   NATO
FAIT CAMINOREAL
ERNE OPEC WHALE
REEL NASA LORAX
```

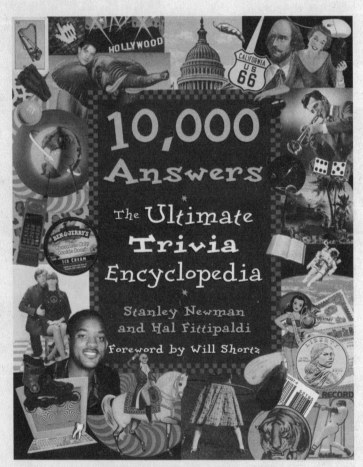